Advanced Praise for Seven Years on Mount Athos

"*Seven Years on Mount Athos* is a book about the power of the will and of know thyself. The power of the will to leave ordinary life and join a community with strict rules. The power of the will to practice self-discipline and live in harmony within the brotherhood, away from family, relatives and friends. Know thyself, the author, a curious and explorative mind, came to question the beliefs with which he grew up, studied and learned and through this process changed himself (rerum causas cognoscere). Eventually the power of the will and know thyself made the author decide to leave the monastic life and return to society. By reading the book one learns to value the important things in life, not waste time on the trivial ones and become a better person."

– Constantinos Saragkas, Greece

"I had the fortune to work with Christos. He is an exceptional conversationalist with clear and peaceful eyes. His very interesting book gives, without any fanaticism, a comprehensive glance to a way of life completely foreign to most of us."

– Nikos Dimitriou, Greece

"So well written, such simple and austere descriptions, so truly flowing out of the soul… Even from the foreword I was 'enchanted' so much that I wanted to read it without a break! What stunned me was the way that the book ends, the last chapter. The 'end' is shocking!"

– Dimitris Toskidis, lifelong friend of the author, Greece

"Once I held the book, it was so interesting and enlightening that I 'literally' swallowed it. Even after so many visits to the Holy Mountain, I admit that I didn't know in detail many aspects of the daily life and the procedures of the monastic order. I also liked the fact that he didn't criticize the brotherhood; he just observed impartially. His writing is formal, careful, and parsimonious. This book will lead the reader to places where I, even after twenty years of regular pilgrimage, observed but didn't have the insight to comprehend."

– Vasilis Chernenko, the Vasilis mentioned in the book, USA

"*Seven Years on Mount Athos* by Christos is a fascinating memoir that takes you on a journey through the secluded world of the Mount Athos monastic community. Christos spent seven years living amongst the monks, and he shares his experiences, from their daily routines to their spiritual practices. The book provides a captivating portrayal of the challenges and rewards of living in a community cut off from the outside world. Overall, it's an engaging read that offers a unique perspective on a mysterious and intriguing way of life. If you enjoy memoirs or are interested in spirituality, this is a book you shouldn't miss."

– Nare Babayan, USA

Christos' book is an extraordinary reading about a man and his adventure to seek the Truth. His internal struggles and the hard decisions he had to take are presented in a very genuine way, while living on Mount Athos for seven years. The life journey of monk Klimis (Christos' name as a monk) in the Holy Mountain are described in a very picturesque way. The authenticity of the descriptions about his everyday tasks as a monk, while trying, at the same time, to live a deeply spiritual life according to the monastery doctrine are truly apocalyptic. Definitely a must read for everyone, believer on not, who wants to know about a man's Odyssey from a western society to a monastic life and back again, the lessons he learned, and how that journey helped him on his pursuit to find happiness and finally salvation."

– Anastasios Katsigiannis, Greece

SEVEN YEARS ON MOUNT ATHOS

THE POWER OF BELIEVING

7YearsOnMountAthos.com

About the author

Christos Palaskas was born in 1981 in Brooklyn, New York. He moved to Greece in 1989 with his deeply religious mother to her hometown of Litohoro, near Mount Olympus. He studied Information and Communication Systems Engineering at the University of the Aegean on the island of Samos and then served seventeen months with distinction as a cadet officer in the Hellenic Special Forces. Following military service, he worked as a computer technician and computer science teacher in Katerini. In 2006, he left his family, relatives, friends, and society to seclude himself in a monastery on "Holy Mountain" Athos. In 2013, he returned to society, settling in the city of Thessaloniki for three years before moving to Seattle, Washington, where he worked as a software engineer for the automotive industry and met his wife, Tiffany. He has two children, Alexander and Arriana. He now strives to improve the world with blockchain technologies, sharing novel ideas with people.

Acknowledgements and Thanks

To my wife Tiffany and my children Alexander and Arriana.

Special thanks to my wife, who supported me on every step of our journey together. She gave me a little golden diary and urged me to start writing my experiences, so I wouldn't forget them. I would probably never have written this account if it were not for her.

Many thanks to Michael Manson, retired professor and father of my friend Josiah. Mike took the time to morph this document into a readable book. He worked intermittently for five months and gave me the idea of making maps of the areas.

Special thanks to Tasos Antsos, who helped me shape my initial notes into a text in Greek.

I want to thank the people that provided pictures for this book, Vangelis Tsintsifas for images 1, 44, 46 and the last 4 images at the end of the book, and George Stamatiou, George Sarkos and Michalis Dimoulas for some of the rest. They did a good job capturing the moment, in a time when I did not care about posterity.

I should also mention and thank all the people who helped with proofreading or offering other feedback: David & Esther Duffy, Marvin Lee, Pete Lymberis, Marat Markarov, Vladimir Stepania, Kosuke Takahashi, Navdeep Singh Thind. I apologize to anyone that I forgot.

GREECE
Thessaloniki
Mt. Olympus
Litochoro
Athos Peninsula
Lesvos
Corfu
AEGEAN SEA
Chios
IONIAN SEA
Chalkida
Patra
ATHENS
Samos
Sparta
Crete
100 km
100 mi
www.mapsopensource.com
Map 1 - Greece

Map 2 - Athos peninsula with some landmarks

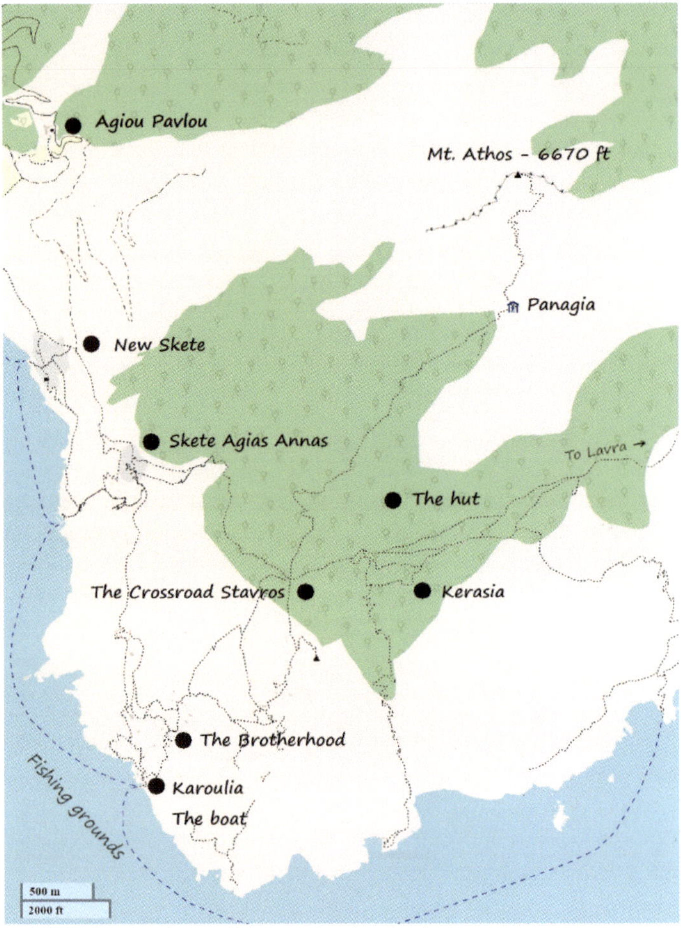

Map 3- The south tip of the peninsula of Athos

Introduction to the English version

The Greek word for monk is "*monachos*", which literally means alone, single. Some other words used to describe this desire of people to leave society to live far away are "*erimitis,*" hermit, meaning a dweller of the desert, and "*isichastis,*" a person who is quiet and silent. This behavior has a very long history.

The first questions that arise on this topic usually are:

- Why do these people abandon society to live an extremely hard life?
- What do they gain?
- What is the day-to-day life of a monk?
- Are there any of the teachings of the monk that are useful to society?
- Is there really "ancient wisdom" that has accumulated to this day?
- What is the source of the strength to endure such self-denial?
- How can someone willingly abstain from life's pleasures?

The author lived for seven-and-a-half years as a monk in a very radical brotherhood, isolated in a monastery on inhospitable rocky terrain, and he then returned to society. This book is his attempt to answer the above questions.

The monastery is located on the Athos peninsula in northeastern Greece. This peninsula has a unique political status. Women are absolutely forbidden. Even male visitors are normally restricted to 134 per day, 120 Orthodox and fourteen non-Orthodox, and their stay is limited to four days. However, there are also special invitations that permit visitors to remain for longer periods. The peninsula has partial autonomy, having its own governor, but relies on the Greek police and coastal forces. There is no electric grid; people use generators or solar power.

The majority of the roughly 2000 inhabitants of the peninsula are monks of the Eastern Orthodox church. They have taken a vow of lifelong celibacy and live a simple life, striving to pay more attention to their spirits than their bodies. They either live in twenty ancient monasteries, the first of which was established in 963 AD, or in one of the many little huts or sketes (monastic communities). Some live alone. Others live in communities of up to 200 monks.

Before the invention of the printing press, these monasteries served society by saving ancient books from extinction by hand-copying them. Countless treasures have been preserved through the centuries in the vaults of the ancient monasteries. For example, one of the monasteries holds a side of Napoleon Bonaparte's tent, which first belonged to the last Bourbon king of France, Louis XVI.

Today, people from around the world, especially from Eastern Europe, visit the peninsula daily, throughout the year. Some seek answers to spiritual questions. Others just crave a few quiet days away from the noise of modern society, technology, and their everyday problems. They stay in a medieval setting and observe ancient rituals and ceremonies.

On the southern part of the peninsula lies the imposing mount of Athos, whose peak is at an altitude of 6,670 feet. The monks that live in that area, called the "Desert," have an even more difficult life, as there are no roads; transportation is facilitated by mules and horses. The land is sloped, making gardening extremely difficult. To make matters worse, water is collected in cisterns from springs through pipes that freeze in the winter. In summer, a scorching sun heats the rocky terrain, making the place most inhospitable.

This is the setting where the heart of this narrative takes place. It starts by exploring the reasons one might be driven to monasticism. It then describes the schedule and everyday life of a monk. Next, through stories and events, the transformation of the young monk is recounted. The narrative culminates in the battle to uproot a belief system embedded within since childhood, leading to the monk's decision to return to society and fight for a normal life against all odds.

After some further years of struggle to forge a new identity, the author accepts himself: the ex-monk who returned to the world, made use of his time as a monk, and never forgot the useful teachings.

Image 1 - The southwest part of Athos peninsula from Agia Anna Skete. Photo with infrared filter.

Preface

by Tasos Antsos, editor of the Greek version

Mount Athos, the garden of Virgin Mary, is a quiet, sacred, and blessed place. It is a place where no matter how many people are with you, you long for holy solitude and time in which you will have the chance for introspection. These are moments during which you wish to extract your pain and your deepest thoughts, which only you know, and which never leave the vicinity of your heart. It is a place where you seek support for your problems. Through prayer, you can unite with God and feel peace in your heart. A prayer in a holy place within the monasteries, or outside in nature.

Even when you are on the boat to Athos and behold the scattered monasteries of the peninsula stretching along the shores of the Gulf of Mount Athos, the sight is so imposing that you feel as if your brain is cleared of negative thoughts. The tranquility of holiness takes their place. This is the time that the grandeur of Mount Athos unfolds. It is a place where you can find serenity.

As the boat continues to sail past the imposing monasteries, you see an area called the "Desert". You see the little skete of Saint Anna, followed by "*Katounakia*," the wonderful "*Karoulia*," Saint Vasilios' skete, "*Kerasia*," and finally "*Kafsokalivia*." These are wild places with cabins perched on the steep slopes of Athos. There live the wildest of the monks, isolated from the rest of the world, away from the conveniences of an organized society. These souls, supposedly dead to the world, go there to live, forgotten by all, a life devoted to God. Humble and noble believers in the value of the soul, they pray for its salvation. People from all walks of life and all levels of education are dead to the world and live as equals helping one another, as their family is now their next-door neighbors.

Some were driven to monasticism after a turning point in their lives, after a sudden forced change, or even a change in their perspective concerning the world and its value. Others were nurtured since childhood on the value of monasticism and the vanity of worldly life. Others were simply meant to be monks; it was purely innate.

On my first visit to the Holy Mount in 2011, I met Christos, then known as Father Klimis (Clement). My first stop was at the monastery of Saint Gregory, after which I went to Katounakia, the final stop. The beauty of the scenery and the simplicity of the hermitages enchanted me. They were not like the majestic monasteries of the north; rather they were quaint farmhouses without comforts or electricity. Unheard of! It was like a journey back in time. Yet, what made a greater impression was the serenity. It was so quiet that I could hear nature, even the flapping of a butterfly's wings. It is one of the few places inhabited by people where nature still dominates.

In this incredibly beautiful paradise, I was blessed to get to know Father Klimis. Even though he was a monk in one of the most radical brotherhoods, his words were balanced, and his mind was open to different views. In this, he was the antithesis of the others, whose views were rigid and who refused to entertain any other point of view. Klimis' character was open to learning, which meant that he was looking for truth through different paths and not strictly through the path his brotherhood showed him. He did not accept all that he heard. He read theological and philosophical books, which finally led him to make the exceedingly difficult decision to leave the Holy Mount.

It was a decision that seemed to come out of the blue when he announced it. I thought Father Klimis was the ideal monk, but he could not live within the bounds of the brotherhood. He was wild in a sense, but willing to accept or refuse. He made his decision to leave after a great deal of thought. Who could have made him change his mind once he had persuaded himself to leave?

After he left the Holy Mount, we kept in touch and fostered a great friendship that has continued to this day. It was through this friendship that he proposed we should write an account of his monastic experiences. We tried to shed light on unknown aspects of monastic life, seen both through the perspective of Klimis the monk and through the mature thought of Christos the civilian. It was a bold decision for Christos to expose himself and to reveal frankly his most secret actions and thoughts. The result is a real confession from a real monk.

Introduction to the Greek version

Since 2013, when "I returned to the world," the thought of writing my experiences from the Holy Mount obsessed me. At times, this feeling was intense, at other times it dissipated. At first, I decided I would defer it to my old age, when I would have more free time. However, a phone call from someone with whom I had lived on Mount Athos for some years made me understand that time erases a lot from memory. It does not erase everything, but it blurs details, stories, situations, feelings, all those things that make a narrative authentic and alive. So, in early 2017, just three-and-a-half years after leaving Mount Athos, I took pen and paper and started writing. I made a list with names, places, events, and words that came to my mind and which I hoped would help me to remember more. Writing exerts a great influence on the human mind. It makes vague thoughts solid. The more I wrote, the more I remembered. Finally, I gave my manuscript to my dear friend Tasos, who edited it into a book in Greek.

For those who do not know the Holy Mount, this book will present a perspective on a monk's real life. It mainly concerns the monks on the south side of the mount, the desert of Athos, which is what I experienced in most of the seven-and-a-half years I was there. From whichever angle you look at it, the people there live a hard life, of which the general public should be aware. In the wider world, some people succeed and acquire wealth, fame, or whatever else they are after. Others, perhaps most, fail. This is also true on Mount Athos; some achieve their goals, and some do not. Some achieve inner peace or spiritual elevation. Others feel an indescribable sensation that makes them immerse themselves in beauty and draw strength from the hardship they experience away from the comforts of city life.

Some readers will probably not agree with my conclusions. They can draw their own conclusions from my narrative. All the facts presented are based on my own experience. I have avoided mentioning names as much as possible. The few exceptions are for people who gave their consent, and I am grateful to them for it.

The aim of my effort is not to emphasize a path that one should follow in life. It is neither meant to support monasticism nor to argue against it. The aim is to demonstrate that a person's free will is invincible. Whoever exerts that will can become free of ways of thinking, religious or not, that kept them imprisoned for decades. The only precondition for one's improvement is to remember what Socrates concluded: "*I only know that I know nothing.*"

I hope readers will find something from my experience that will help them discover their own "truth," their own path. I stress the unique path, because I do not believe that there is a single path for everyone. I have met happy people, "saintly people" I dare say, people who emit joy and energy and positive vibes to all around them, people you are glad to be with, who do or do not identify with a specific religion. These people all have their strengths and their weaknesses. One can focus on the positive things they project, or one can search for their flaws. Doing the latter will diminish you as well, whereas doing the former will add to your own strength.

Christos Palaskas

(Former monk Klimis)

July 2018

Image 2 - A hut in Karoulia, and some prickly pears.

Image 3 - Rocks on the tin roof to keep it from getting torn by the wind. Karoulia.

Image 4 - The author at Karoulia.

Image 5 - The author at Karoulia.

Chapter 1. A strict upbringing

The beginning is half of every work.

Plato, Laws 753e

It is said that the childhood years are the most important for shaping one's personality. My brother and I grew up in a strictly religious family. Our mother belonged to the Greek Orthodox Church of the Julian Calendar, a radical division of the main Church of Greece. My father was not deeply religious, especially in comparison to my mother. It was not easy to belong to this church, and my mother tried to control everything in our lives according to the rules and traditions of that church. This, believe me, made life difficult.

I was born in New York in 1981. My father, a US citizen but also an immigrant from Greece, went back to his hometown Litohoro, to find a wife. That town lies under the shadow of Mount Olympus, the birthplace of the twelve gods of Greek mythology. It is a magical place, as it is also close to a beautiful beach.

After the wedding and the honeymoon, they moved back to the US. They had two children, my brother and me. We attended a Greek private school and led a fairly normal life. But something was missing from my mother's life. She started obsessing with religion, perhaps as a way to fill an internal gap. After nine years of living in New York, she finally could not take it anymore and had to move back to Greece to be with her family.

Father sold his business and house and followed us there. He was doing his best to keep the family happy. He built a house for us, next to his mother-in-law's. In addition, he tried for some time to start a business in Greece, but he was not successful. His American mentality was not compatible with life in Greece. So, my parents made a peculiar arrangement. He would go back to the US and work there, then return for several months every year or two to visit us. We were raised almost solely by my mother.

She continually applied all the teachings of her church to us. She read passages of the Holy Bible and the lives of saints during every meal. She took us to church every Sunday and for every great celebration, unless we had school that day. All my activities and accomplishments, such as mountain climbing, running marathons, serving in the Special Forces of the Hellenic Army, parachuting, and even my graduation from university, were, for her, mundane and insignificant things.

For a child, this upbringing seemed a great burden. We could not engage in activities normal for other children. We could not go to other children's name-day parties because they celebrated according to the new calendar. We could not even go to their birthday parties, as our church did not consider birthdays as being of value. So, we grew up isolated from other children of our age.

My mother used to say that what I had to do was to become a monk to save my soul. Our church, like many others, claimed that only their teachings represented the true faith. The only road to salvation was through them. Therefore, we had to travel long distances to attend church services that proclaimed this dogma. This is the way we were brought up. This was my mother's faith, and she did what she believed was right.

Image 6 - The monastery of Simonos Petra.

Chapter 2. Out of the nest

Ask not what your country can do for you;
ask what you can do for your country.

John F. Kennedy

My admission to the University of the Aegean and the subsequent move from home helped expand my awareness of life. I left my hometown Litohoro and lived on my own for the first time on the distant island of Samos. Contact with other students and the discussions I had with them introduced me to different points of view and theories. At last, I had the freedom to read books with content different from the books I had read up to then. I devoured ancient Greek writers and philosophers, along with books about other religions - mainly Oriental – and I saw films. All this made me start to wonder about, although not yet question, my convictions.

Could I really question my mother's teachings, which were etched so deep in my mind? These were teachings that were forced on the young mind with the threat of expulsion from the house, accompanied by some force, if I didn't ultimately agree with them. I could in no way accept that most of the things I had learned as a child were simply wrong, especially when I lived with her after my studies. She could control me; I had been trained to listen to her voice. No matter how much she taught me, and even though I accepted everything, I still had questions to ask, particularly after university. Deep inside me, something was always burning. I was not sure what the truth was.

Even then, beside my mother, I tried to find answers to the questions which popped up in my brain. Does God exist? Do we have an eternal soul? Is our church really the only path to salvation? What makes us so special, compared to the billions of other people? We did not use smartphones then, nor social networks, but I tried to read magazines, such as *National Geographic*, to find answers. However, no matter what I discovered, the new thoughts crashed against the wall of my insecurity. I was not sure what the truth was.

Being a member of a church of the Old Calendar, I was not allowed to go to churches which adhered to the New Calendar. This schism occurred in the Eastern Orthodox church in 1924, when the council decided to adopt the new Gregorian Calendar over the old Julian Calendar for ecclesiastical use, and declared March 10th, 1924, as March 23rd. For historical context, the Julian calendar was established by the Emperor of Rome, Julius Caesar in 46 BC and took effect on January 1st, 45 B.C. A Greek astronomer, Sosigenes of Alexandria, was one of the designers. Over the centuries, people observed that the solstice and equinox were slipping back, which meant that the calendar in use was inadequate. They estimated that the solar year was 365.2425 days, instead of 365.25 of the Julian calendar. Thus, Pope Gregory XIII introduced a new rule for leap years:

"To be a leap year, the year number must be divisible by four – except for end-of-century years, which must be divisible by 400."

So, every 400 years, the two calendars grow apart by three days. Scientists today believe that the solar year is closer to 365.24219 days, and it varies a bit, which means that we will lose a day in about 3000 years. I'm sure someone will figure something out by then!

Back to the schism; the country had already adopted the new calendar for political use in 1923. Other Orthodox countries, such as Russia and Serbia still use the Gregorian for political purposes, while keeping the Julian for religious matters. But in Greece the decision was not unanimous and some bishops with their supporters seceded, keeping the old, even though they knew that it was not astronomically correct. It was another way of showing their disproval of the Pope and the Catholic church, and the movement of Ecumenism. By not accepting the calendar that bore the Pope's name (Gregory XIII), another distinction was created.

That is why I did not attend church, not even once, during my time at university. Besides, I did not feel the need to be at church, because a young man's life was so full.

Those five years at college started shaping my personality. I made extraordinarily strong friendships that last to this day. We still trust each other with almost everything. It was also a period when my passion for nature was defined. Mountaineering, rock climbing, running, fishing, snorkeling, and sailing were activities that helped define who I was becoming, on my own, away from the house. But the next school I had to attend was the Army. That was the school that taught me the significance of discipline.

The Army

In Greece, every able male citizen must serve in the Armed Forces, either Army, Navy, or Air Force. At that time, the mandatory period of service was twelve months. Growing up listening to stories from my grandfather, who was a World War II veteran, struck a chord in my heart, a craving for valor and honor. I decided that, as I was going to serve for twelve months anyway, I might as well make some use of that time and learn something more. Thus, I volunteered to join the Special Forces, which was much harder than the regular army. We would learn some additional skills, but, most importantly, we would learn how to discipline ourselves. About 1,200 young men were recruited initially, with the intent to keep only about 800 after one month. To that end, the drill sergeants tried to pressure 400 of us to quit voluntarily, so that only the best would go on to the units. They would wake us up at 5 am, forcing us to shave and make our beds in fifteen minutes, work us out for hours, and then assign us some physical labor. We were taught to shout loudly when responding, and to hold our heads high to build self-confidence. Lunch and dinner were served at the mess hall, but because its capacity was only 300, we had to finish eating in fifteen minutes, scarfing down food, before we were out on the field again. That was the best moment for the sergeants to press us hard, when we had full stomachs.

I was in top physical condition at the time, because, after my university graduation, I was working out daily, preparing for the call from the Army. Thus, I was in the top tier in all the competitions. Also, I had a college degree, which resulted in my being selected to serve as a Cadet officer. That meant I would have to remain in the Army an extra five months, but I would get paid and could live outside the barracks. I could also attend many of the Special Forces training schools, which would not have been an option had I remained a private.

After graduating from the month-long Special Forces boot camp, about a hundred cadet candidates were shipped to the island of Crete to attend the Cadet Officers school, which would last four months. Only twenty-five of us made it to serve the Special Forces as Cadet officers, while the rest were assigned to regular army units. This was the first time I realized that life was not fair, and that people with power and connections could overtly promote their children's rise in place of other, more capable men.

When the colonel, something akin to the headmaster of the school, interviewed us (about 360 men), I was ranked third and promoted to staff sergeant, being responsible for a company of roughly 170 men. I had to make sure that things were carried out in a fair manner; for example, I ensured that everyone had equal opportunities for leaves and vacations. I was also responsible for executing the captain's assignments by dividing the work fairly among my four platoons. These responsibilities were very new to me, considering that a few months before, I had still been in college, a young man with virtually no responsibilities. It was such a stressful period that I developed a constant stomachache. But I managed to graduate from the school, ranking sixth out of the 344 men that graduated.

After graduation, I was transferred to a Marine Corps battalion in the beautiful city of Chalkida. More responsibilities were given to me, besides being the leader of my platoon. I was assigned to the armory, which meant I had to keep track of every rifle, pistol, and piece of equipment that was going in and out of the warehouse. It was a nightmare! There, I learned to lead by example. From observing my superiors, I realized that I would be happy to serve under some officers but despised others. Thus, I tried to copy the actions and traits of those that I liked. They were humble but respectable, and they led by example. They could stoop down to the level of the private and show exactly what needed to be done. I also learned how important it is to listen. Sometimes people do not need answers; they just need someone to whom they can open their hearts and share their problems.

I also attended the Basic Parachuting school, where we performed static line jumps from airplanes and learned to overcome our fears and trust our equipment and training. In addition, I completed the Unorthodox Warfare school, finishing third in the class, where, among other things, I learned how the body functions without extended periods of sleep. Miles and miles of walking during the night, with no sleep and minimal food, carrying full gear and weapons, taught me that when the mind wills, the body obeys.

Overall, my service in the army was an amazing and dynamic time that taught me a great deal. It was, after college, the second real world experience I had, and it prepared me as a young adult to enter society. Strong friendships were formed there, too, people with whom I endured much in training. Most importantly, it exposed me to a variety of people, good and bad, unlike college, where everyone was pretty much of similar social status. My military service surely prepared me to endure the physical hardships of life in a remote monastery.

Chapter 3. The decision to become a monk

Man is a prison where the soul remains free.

Victor Hugo

A young man I knew from our church abandoned the world and went to a monastery to become a monk. After a few years, I visited him. It had never crossed my mind that I would become a monk, although my mother had encouraged me all those years to do so. I liked the serenity and peace inherent in a monk's life, but I remember how much I was sorry for all those young men who were secluded in a monastery. They did not have the freedom to leave whenever they pleased. How did they find the strength to renounce all worldly joys? I felt sorry for them.

Yet, monks are good at speaking, especially when they meet a young man who asks a lot of questions. They try to persuade him to follow them. So, they started telling me things that may seem untrue to me today, but then, mindful of my mother's preaching, I received everything as true and serious. They spoke to me about how difficult and unjust the external world is, and how God would punish this world of Satan and annihilate it. The end was near, only a few years away. Only through prayer and repentance could we manage to approach God to save our souls. These teachings, complemented by my mother's preaching, somehow convinced me that the end of the world was near, that a terrible ruler would appear and take dominion over the earth and persecute all Christians. That belief made the struggle to succeed in society less worthwhile.

They were right about prayer. It is cleansing when it is carried out in the right way. It helps you forgive those that wronged you. It conditions your subconscious mind to find solutions. It helps bolster your resolve. They were right about other things, too, some of which I find true even today. In particular, I learned many useful things about my life and my daily routine. I learned to see God inside others. We are all children of God, and God is inside each one of us. We are all equal in the eyes of God, and we should not discriminate against anyone. I learned to face my fellow humans with love and understanding, without any hostility and antagonism. They used to say we had to hate the sin but not the sinner. Even the worst people were deceived by Satan, and still deserved our love. I also learned about a healthy diet and the value of fasting for the spirit and the body as well.

They also recommended books, which I read, such as those of Nikodemus of Mount Athos, a scholarly monk of the 18th century. These books glorified monasticism and disapproved of secular society, i.e., starting families and raising children. The books brought up rules and laws in numbers that would overwhelm a modern person who wanted to follow them. It seemed impossible to abide by those rules and yet remain in society.

From then on, I visited the monks several times over the next two years. I came to wonder which path was right; to stay in the world, follow a career, get married, and have a family, or to confine myself in a monastery to calm my heart and soul? Which path should I follow? The answer was always the same: remain an active member of society. However, something tormented me. I was at a crossroads, and I had to choose which road to take.

At the monastery I visited, there was a monk-priest who stimulated my interest. From our discussions, I realized that he had considerable knowledge of math, physics, chemistry, and mechanics. When I asked him certain questions, he thought quite a bit before responding, and in my eyes, he seemed to be a responsible and reasonable person. Many times, he answered my question after hours, working through the issue in his mind. For example, if I asked him why the church forbade premarital sexual relationships, he tried to answer from a physical perspective and not through the prism of church laws. He said that a young person had to focus on other things first, such as education, and not waste energy, emotions, and time before being ready to commit. If I asked about the fasting and the reason they didn't eat meat, he would reply that it pertained to the negative effects of eating meat on the body, and the positive effects of allowing ample time for the digestive system to process. Through this responsible behavior, he slowly gained my trust. He sometimes visited me at my house, apparently urged to do so by my mother. He always talked to me about spiritual elation and the highest levels of spirituality that could be reached through "mental" prayer. This is a type of prayer in which you remain calm and control your breathing as you repeat the phrase 'Lord Jesus Christ, Son of God, have mercy on me,' or something similar, hundreds of times. This prayer will be discussed in more detail later.

I heard two voices within me. The one that told me to seclude myself in a monastery grew strong. It overcame logic. However, logic still had a voice and prevented me from committing myself to monastic life, using my human wishes and needs as arrows in its quiver. I definitely needed advice from somebody I trusted, and there was no one at hand other than the monk-priest. So, when I asked how to find what God's will was, he replied that I should pray for three consecutive days and the answer would appear.

I do not know exactly how it happened, but the answer did indeed come on the third day. I believed that it was God's reply, although it may have been the result of my psyching myself up. It may have been a defense mechanism my mind created to escape from all the pressure I felt because of my dilemma - a response from my subconscious mind. I feared that, if I stayed in society, I was going to betray my values and all that I had been taught by my mother for my whole life. Above all, I feared that I would betray God's law, of which my understanding, in reality, was only the nominal interpretation of church laws.

Driving home after work on the third day of my prayer, while I was listening to Byzantine music, I suddenly felt a crushing weight on my heart, from the realization that I was a sinner, and I burst into tears. I felt that this world was fragile, without value. It was not worth fighting to win a place in it. The words of Ecclesiastes echoed in my mind: "Vanity of vanities; all is vanity". The conviction came to my mind then, apparently out of nowhere, that I was going to the Mount to become a monk. At once, I felt peace within my heart. The pressure of my dilemma had vanished, and my soul became tranquil. I had made my decision.

Needless to say, it made my mother incredibly happy when I announced my decision to her. And this proves how strong faith is. How could a mother who was about to part with her twenty-five-year-old son forever be so happy? She had never been happier in her life. This was her faith, and she considered that this would be the best option for me.

I also called my father to announce my decision. He replied that I was the only one in control of my life and that the decision was solely mine. If that was what I wanted to do, then I should do it. On the other hand, my brother was totally indifferent. He apparently had his own problems, his own decisions to make, so he did not take much notice of it. For one reason or another, we never really got along. Those three were the only people who knew about my decision, and they kept it to themselves.

I quit my job and sold my car and motorcycle. I did not care about anything anymore. The only thing I wanted was to leave the world and go live in the serenity of the Holy Mount, to calm my heart and live in the path of God. I later discovered, however, that serenity is an inner state that you can achieve anywhere, in the busy heart of Manhattan or in the isolation of the Sahara Desert.

Image 7 - Stavronikita monastery with Mt. Athos in the background.

Image 8 - Skete Agia Anna.

Chapter 4. First impressions

Only those who have not lived life are content with it.

Albert Camus

April 14th, 2006 was a Friday. It was the day that I severed all ties with the larger world, my family, and my friends. I did not take much more than some clothes with me. There was no need to take anything to remember, to immerse myself in the shibboleths of sentimentality, reminders of the past. I felt so light; nothing was a burden. There were no worries or responsibilities. I was reborn! I only took a crate of tinned feta cheese and a bag of lemons as an offering to the brotherhood. That was all. I did not need anything else.

Nobody knew where I was going besides my mother, father, and brother. Nobody else. Not even my uncle, who lived next door, or even my closest friends. What did we want to hide from them? Why all that secrecy? Perhaps, I feared that every effort on the part of the others to comprehend that stage of my life would have produced a terribly flawed outline of it. Maybe they would try to dissuade me, but I was sure about the decision I had made! We just told everyone that I was going on a trip to America to visit my father.

Although we were ostensibly going to the airport, my mother and brother took me to the port of Ouranoupoli, and there I bid farewell to them forever. It was a minor death; I was never going to see them again! However, I did not feel bad. I was going to be reborn into a new life, one that was more spiritual and more substantial.

That afternoon I arrived at Katounakia. I stood at the port and looked up high. Above me stood Mount Athos, imposing and proud. It stood there as a welcoming beacon. Within its view I was going to spend the rest of my life, and if I were blessed, I would find the peace I longed for there. My feelings of guilt began to disappear, those feelings that were locked inside me from all those years of preaching. It was not the first time I gazed at Athos, but it was the first time that I observed it closely. At last! This was my home. I had to learn everything about it, which was what I tried to do in the years I lived there.

I followed the path. The new path of my life started with 2000 steps up to my cell. I carried ninety pounds on my back, from sea level to a height of 985 feet, but I could not care less. This was undertaken gladly because I looked forward to starting my new life.

The ten monks who lived there greeted me warmly. The elder was neither the eldest in age nor the foremost in monasticism but was elected because he was the most scholarly of the group. I quickly adjusted to their program, since all these things were familiar to me. I had visited them several times in the past. There is an old saying that the zeal and eagerness of a novice monk, or "*dokimos*," as the monks call them, is as big as Mount Athos. As time progresses the zeal dwindles, so by the time of ordination the zeal is barely the size of a little hill. This saying proved absolutely true for me.

Image 9 - My new home at the top of the hill, as seen from the seaport.

The place I was going to live for the rest of my life was not one of those majestic monasteries that come to mind when you think about the Holy Mount. It was a humble farmhouse that did not remind you of a monastery. Its church was humble too, a small room inside the house with a few icons. Naturally, there was no electricity. It was an old farmhouse belonging to another era. Outside, there was a huge veranda with a view of the Aegean. At dawn, you could see the shadow of Athos in front of you as a perfect pyramid. Nature dominated everywhere, and we lived in perfect harmony with it.

Image 10 - Mt Athos' shadow cast on the sea at sunrise.

I was shown to my room. It was a 6x6 foot cell. They really call the rooms cells, *kellion*, as in prison cells, not as in the biological term. I could almost touch both walls by stretching my arms. The bed was a wooden plank with four legs, and on it was a woolen blanket. The bed was barely wide enough so that you would not fall off when you turned over. In the summer, it was so hot that I removed the blanket and slept right on the plank. There was a cupboard on the wall for me to put my clothes in. On the cupboard there was a human skull. A real skull! It belonged to the former owner of the cell, a monk who was killed in 1996, while he was digging in the mountain for the construction of a new storehouse. There were human skulls and bones in every monk's cell, a constant reminder of the day we would die and a way to help us avoid impure thoughts and deeds. It was a constant reminder that our time was running out, and at the end we were going to be judged for our actions. They taught us that wasting time was a spiritual disease and that staying the same equaled decline. We should always improve ourselves on the path we had chosen to follow. The goal for a monk of Mount Athos is to improve himself in preparation for the final judgement by God; to reach the state of *apathia*. Any help a monk provides to humanity is a corollary effect, as people observe their virtues and learn by their example or converse with them. By definition, a monk is dead to the world, and the world is dead to him.

In the larger society, the goal could be to become a better person, a better member of society, and to help humanity. The most common way is to start a family, working daily to improve your relationship with your spouse and your children and to raise children with the foundation to ensure they become fully integrated members of society. Another way is to develop a career that serves people and improves their quality of life. Or one can become an active participant in a church or charity. The common element is the significance of time. You cannot advance by wasting time in non-productive activities. Back to my cell, though. After a while I got used to the skull and bones and hardly noticed them anymore. They simply became a part of the decoration. But by then, you had developed a habit of not wanting to waste time.

Image 11 - Human skulls and bones were a common display on Athos' dwellings, as a reminder of mortality.

On my second day there, my elder gave me the monks' cap, which I had to wear all the time, even when I was sleeping. He also delegated two errands to me. One was to ring a bell three to four times a day, before our gatherings, and the other was to keep a part of the house clean. My zeal was so great that I did both perfectly. You might say that I did not do anything great. I just rang a bell periodically and cleaned part of the house. Later, I did not even clean anymore, and even took off my cap at night. In time, I was assigned other jobs, such as the grooming and the general maintenance of the mules. I also learned the art of Byzantine icon painting, and specifically the technique of the Cretan school.

Forty days after my arrival at the monastery, and because I was perfect in all the tasks I had undertaken, my elder gave me the *zostiko*, which is the familiar black garment, like a robe, which monks wear tied with a leather belt around the waist. This garment symbolizes the shroud with which dead people are wrapped before burial. The meaning was that we were dead for the outside world and that this was our new life. The belt is made of leather and goes around the waist and the vital internal organs, which was believed to be where the sex drive arose, specifically from the kidneys. Although I understood even then that this thinking was factually wrong, the symbolism acted as a deterrent in the mind of the faithful, and the body obeyed.

When I saw myself wrapped in the *zostiko*, I fully realized what I was doing. The great pressure that had borne down on me previously because of my dilemma brought with it pain and continual stress. All this accumulated despair had led me to make a decision, one that I was unsure would be the right one in the end. In the back of my mind, I knew that I had not yet given a pledge. I was just a novice and could get up and leave at any time. Conversely, the brotherhood itself could send me away if I became unbearable. With these thoughts, I calmed myself down.

The pledge should have come after one year, but I put it off. It was only after four years that I took the "*rasoefhi*," an ordaining that is normally given after a year of a novice monk's confinement.

At the stage of *rasoefhi*, the novice is given another ceremonial black garment, called *raso*, to wear over the *zostiko* garment when he is at church. This covers all the body and has exceedingly long and wide sleeves. There is also a garment for the head, which reaches the waist or even lower, called *epanokalimafho*. This symbolizes the two wings of an angel, since according to the ecclesiastic bibliography, monks will replace Lucifer's order in Heaven. At this time, the monk is given his new name. This procedure symbolizes his death for the world and his birth as a new person with a new opportunity to purify his soul.

To reach the final stage, at least three more years are required, and only if his elder and brotherhood decide that the monk is ready. He then pledges oaths to stay in the brotherhood for all his life. In addition, he gets his final garment, an apron filled with red symbols, the Great Schema, and a woolen vest covered with embroidered crosses, the *polistavrio.*

I remained at stage one for four years. Was the reason that I never felt a spiritual connection with my elder, despite my respect for him, or was it that I was simply uncertain? The mind can play great tricks on you. The bottom line may have been that my misery and accumulated despair led me to make a hurried decision about my confinement on the Mount, and now, after so many years of peace, I slowly realized that it was a mistake. I was not sure whether I wanted to undertake the responsibility of the *rasoefhi* pledge.

Finally, in the fourth year from the day I entered the monastery, I decided to become a monk. The elder and the other members of the brotherhood were very pleased with this decision. Also, they had to find a suitable name for me. The elder thought that I should be given the name Klimis to commemorate and honor the brotherhood's founder, who had died in 1992. The second in hierarchy, the oldest, who was the brotherhood's gardener and cook, recommended the name Hrisostomos, meaning *golden mouth*, in honor of a former elder. My own recommendation was the name Dionysius, who was the patron saint of my home village and beloved mountain Olympus. Then of course my elder pointed out, in his own way, that there was no democracy in the brotherhood, and the only say was his. However, when I saw that the second in hierarchy insisted and did not give up, I kept insisting too. After several disagreements, I finally suggested we should draw lots about the name, so that God would decide. Without this arrangement, I would not become a monk. This was something unheard of, but, pressured by my threat, they accepted it. Therefore, I wrote the names on three pieces of paper, and they told me to go in front of the cross inside the chapel and say the prayer: "Dear God, may your will be done and not ours." The piece of paper that was drawn had the name Klimis, making my elder incredibly happy. I had to accept this as God's will.

Why was it so important for me to choose my own name? Even the first name we get is from our parents and thus we have no agency in its choice. Was it a struggle to retain a little piece of autonomy in a life otherwise totally defined by others? A small revolution against the rules and traditions that we lived by?

I must note here that they never checked the pieces of paper to see that all the names were written, either before the drawing or afterwards. They trusted that I was telling the truth. This was generally true with most matters: lies were simply unthinkable. As monks we were taught never to lie, cheat, or be dishonest. God watched everything you did, said, and thought, and you would be judged, even for your innermost thoughts. We were taught to be true to our faith at any cost, even our lives. To strengthen our resolve, we were given many examples of martyrs who preferred death to denying their faith. In larger society, cheating and deceiving might get you a long way, but even if you aren't caught, your inner peace and conscience inevitably suffer. People you deceive will distance themselves from you, so you will always need to find new friends to deceive. With no real friendships, loneliness will start eating at you.

We were taught that a lie generates more lies to cover it. A lie is a contradiction of fact. You have to create a fake world where that lie becomes real. When you are unable to fake reality any further, you will be exposed and ridiculed. You will also waste energy maintaining your fantasy worlds, causing your mind unrest. When speaking what you believe to be true, you do not have to fabricate facts. You can still be wrong, of course, but you do not have to dissemble.

Image 12 – The young mules Chelidonis and Kastanis are carrying the chestnuts we collected from the forest.

Chapter 5. Everyday life on Mount Athos

A happy life consists in tranquility of mind.

Cicero

- *The prayer schedule*

Time on Mount Athos is calculated in the Byzantine way. At sunset, in all seasons of the year, the clock shows midnight. This means that someone has to check the time in relation to the position of the sun every five to ten days, using graphs or looking at the position of the sun, because sunset does not occur at the same time every day of the year. The same brother was responsible for waking up all the brotherhood at night, one hour before the service gathering, so that we could all say our personal prayers. Those consisted of 100-150 *kneelings* and 1500 repetitions of a two second prayer while performing the symbol of the cross on your body. This brother was also responsible for accounting for everyone's presence at the gathering, so if somebody was absent, he investigated his whereabouts and why he was missing. I performed these duties from the day I arrived until the day I left. This was not at all easy, as I had to wake up every day six hours after sunset, in other words at about three o'clock in the morning in the summer and at midnight in winter. It follows that our sleep time was limited.

The duration of the service in church ranged from three to five hours, depending on whether we had a *liturgy* service at the end. If there was a special service devoted to the saint of the day, or if it was Saturday or Sunday, we had to read and chant following the *Great Clock*, taking turns. This Great Clock was a book with prayers and psalms we had in the monastery. The edition of our Clock was from the early 20th century. The order with which we read the Clock was determined by the *Typikaris*, the person responsible for the monastic order.

On all other days, we remained silent for three hours and prayed in a meditative manner, repeating the mental prayer "Lord Jesus Christ, Son of God, have mercy on us" 4800 times! We had rosary ropes with 300 knots that assisted in counting. (16 times 300 is 4800). But on all occasions, we ended the service by praying for ten minutes for all the people who had contributed or sent offerings or money to us. It was our way of saying thank you.

When we finished our prayers, we could rest for three hours. As soon as the three hours had passed, I had to ring the bell again, indicating the beginning of our work duties. So, sleep time was limited to three hours in the evening and three hours in the morning after church. As for myself, I did not say my personal prayer in the night but after my morning rest, in order to sleep more at night. Therefore, I managed to sleep for four hours in a row and two more hours in the morning. Still, the sleep was not enough, and a feeling of tiredness was permanent. Every physical activity required extra willpower to start. Once you started it, though, it became easier.

- *The work schedule*

Each one of us had a main duty and some other chores. The main duty of the brotherhood was icon making, using the Byzantine technique. We only used temperas made from egg yolk, vinegar, and natural colors from minerals and stones. Some of the icon boards were prepared by my elder before the stage of painting. He used a special technique called *tsukaniko*, engraving symbols and crosses on the gold plate of the icon. The word *tsukaniko* derives from the sound that the little hammer makes when it engraves the gold plate, *tsuk, tsuk, tsuk*. Some monks did not wish to learn the art of iconography and did other jobs, such as gardening, rosaries, necklaces, and making little bracelets with the Virgin Mary's tears – a seed from a local plant that we cultivated.

All these were the main jobs with which we occupied ourselves. We had to work four to six hours a day on these jobs except Sundays and holidays, of which there were plenty throughout the year. The income from selling our productions was used to buy necessities.

Image 13 - One of the icons I painted on gold plated boards with egg tempera.

Besides the main duties, we had chores, or *diakonimata* (services). The whole property was divided and allocated to each one of us, excluding, of course, the elderly, and we were responsible for the general cleaning. Normally, sweeping weekly was enough. Then, there was the so-called *Vourdounaris* service, which was being responsible for the mules. I accepted that service from the second year onwards, and I had to feed them, keep their stables clean, take care of the saddles, and buy the clover and barley for the year. I also had to search for them if they did not return after being set free to find pasture. For me, the care of the mules was not a chore, it was a pleasure; it was a good reason to get away from the monastery and it gave me the opportunity to care for another life. Pets and animals were always dear to me.

Image 14 - Taking care of the mules was one of the tasks that gave me joy.

Image 15 - Life was hard, as manual labor was required for the simplest of tasks, like carrying branches to burn the oven.

Another chore was the carrying of goods from and to the port. If the weather permitted, a ship docked twice a day, bringing groceries, different materials, and visitors. Usually, the younger brothers went down to the port, especially whoever expected to receive something or meet a visitor. Most of the times it was me. I went with great eagerness. It was a way to avoid icon making, which was tiring to the back and to the eyes. Also, it was a good way to get some exercise because I had to descend and ascend 2000 stairs, along with loading and unloading the mules. The port was also a place for monks to gather, our equivalent of a coffeehouse. Naturally, coffeehouses did not exist on Athos. The port was simply the place where we learned news from other brotherhoods and from the outside world. As we were used to seeing only men with beards and black robes, we liked to study the clothes and faces of the visitors. Our eyes could see colors besides the black of the robes, the gray of the rocks, the blue of the sky and sea, and the green of the trees.

Doing the dishes was one more chore we did in weekly shifts. The same person was always the cook's assistant. He had to clean vegetables, peel potatoes and onions, clean fish, knead, and bake the weekly bread. The cook was so experienced after doing it for sixty years that he would place the right amount of wood in the stove and leave. At the right time, like clockwork, the fire would die down and the food was ready, right on cook's schedule!

Image 16 - The dock, where we socialized while waiting for the ship.

Image 17 - Loading the mules was a delicate process, as any imbalance could be disastrous.

We also had to undertake technical duties, such as the plumbing, mechanical jobs (such as the maintenance of the motor of the boat), construction, maintenance, or even sewing work. Of course, we had to do everything on our own. Even when someone was ill, we concocted home-made medications and tried to make him feel better. Of course, when someone was terribly ill, he was taken to a hospital, outside Mount Athos. But there were some who did not want to leave but only wished to recover alone, which was not always successful. I had to remove stitches myself a few times and clean wounds on humans and mules.

Performing all these jobs, especially the ones considered "humiliating," such as cleaning toilets or stables, given that we had to obey orders and not perform them on our free will, was an exercise to control our pride and become humbler. Everything in monasticism is honed through eons to bring the final outcome: a perfect monk.

- *The schedule of meals*

There was great discipline in eating. We could not eat whenever we wanted, not even a small morsel. On top of that, we always had to eat together at the dining table, partaking of whatever the cook had prepared. The feeling of hunger was constant. We always ate silently, listening to the elder read sermons by Saint John of the Climax (Ladder), the *Limonario*, or some other ancient book. There was no hurry. We waited patiently for the last one to finish his meal or the elder to finish the chapter he was reading.

The meals were served either once or twice a day. Almost half the days of the year we ate only once. This type of day is called "*ninth*" because the one meal is served on the ninth hour, by Byzantine time, that is to say three hours before sunset. On these days, the food was cooked without oil and other fats, usually just beans or rice with vegetables boiled only in water. We also had fruit, nuts, and bread. Then, about fifty days of the year, we had two meals, with fish, salad, fruit and, sometimes, a small dessert. Other times we had a meal comprised of potatoes, onions, and a slice of cheese. The rest days of the year we could eat the same type of fat-free food we had on the "*ninth*" days, but twice. Finally, on almost all weekends, we could have a small glass of wine. On these "good" days, we ate as much as we wanted because the food was tastier and more fulfilling, and because the next meal was twenty-two hours away.

- *The "mental" hour*

At 7.00 by Byzantine time, we retired to our cells for an hour of mental prayer. The cell was darkened, and everyone was quiet. Our attention was centered on our heart, and we cleared our minds of any other thought. Sometimes we would repeat the prayer of Jesus, "Lord Jesus Christ son of God, have mercy on me," keeping a steady pace of breath. Other times, we would just meditate on a theme from Jesus' life, e.g., while He was on the cross. We spoke no words, trying instead to feel the magnitude of sacrifice and our own sinfulness. Another meditative guide was to visualize your heart or inner self as a castle, clearing all thoughts. You would lock yourself inside the castle and consider any thoughts that came to you as arrows from an enemy outside the castle. As you let the arrows hit the wall, but bounce off, likewise you did not engage or answer any of your thoughts. If you kept doing this, it became easier and easier to clear your head from thoughts and find peace.

This was not easy at all, especially in the beginning. Sometimes the hour would pass quickly, but sometimes you peeked at the clock thinking it was almost time, when only ten minutes had gone by. The elder would guide the younger monks in these meditations, telling them which ways they should go or should not go. We were also encouraged to shed tears, as it is cleansing to the soul. They said it "softens the heart."

The purpose of this mental prayer was to come closer to divinity and finally reach a state of existence with no passions, lusts, or urges. It was called "*apathia*." People that reach that state are said to have complete control over their thoughts. They are not afraid of dying anymore, do not care much about food or other bodily necessities, and do not become angry or offended. They have a connection with the Divine that fills their hearts with serenity and peace. They are totally satisfied.

- *Vespers and end-of-day routines*

At 8.00 by Byzantine time, we gathered at the church for the evening prayer, which lasted fifty minutes. If it was a "*ninth*" day we had our daily meal after the evening prayer. Otherwise, we returned to work. The work stopped at 11.00 by Byzantine time in both cases. After this time, we either had free time (on ninth days) or we had dinner (the rest of the days). During our free time, thirty to seventy-five minutes before sunset, we could attend to our personal hygiene. I also had to feed the mules and attend to some other small chores. My favorite moment was when we sat on the veranda and enjoyed the wonderful sunset. I have never seen such a gorgeous sunset anywhere else. The sun cast its last beams over the surrounding sea, creating a golden path. Then it dipped behind the mountains at the horizon, leaving a feeling of fulfilment for the day and hope for the next one. Perhaps it was this period of relaxation, after a day that was tiring both mentally and physically, that made it so special. It was the moment when the mind was clear of thoughts and allowed the unhindered eyes to behold, in awe, nature. It was a moment of prayer for the blessing of God.

Image 18 - The view from the monastery was gorgeous. I would just stare at the sea for a long time.

Image 19 - The sun would dip into the horizon, giving us beautiful sunsets.

At 12.15, i.e., a quarter after sunset, we assembled at church for the after-supper prayer, *apodeipnon*, which lasted about a half hour. When it was over, we formed a circle, bowed our heads deeply and touched the ground with our hands, facing the middle of the church while asking loudly for forgiveness from each other. No matter how we might have wronged each other during the day, we would not allow it to linger during the night. Then one by one, starting from the second in hierarchy, we would exit the church bowing to the elder and kissing his hand.

The bowing was symbolic and synergistic with humility. I think that by repetition, it became easier to apologize when I was wrong, even to this day. We were taught that to be the last in this world is to become the first in Heaven. Humility is based on the fact that you are a sinner, and innocent Jesus has paid the price for your sins. Pride is a Satanic quality and should be avoided.

In larger society, pride is often considered a virtue. However, I believe that it is an impediment to our improvement. The humbler you are, the more likely it is you will learn something. Pride can permeate our actions, without realizing it. Being an expert in one area does not make you an expert in other areas. If pride bloats your self-esteem, you might not take advice that would be to your advantage. "I only know that I know nothing," said Socrates, humbling himself in front of the infinite knowledge that existed and still exists in the Universe. The more you learn, the more you see how limited your knowledge is. You realize that there are higher levels of understanding than you had imagined.

Back to our monastic schedule! After the prayer and asking for forgiveness, the day actually ended, and we had to be silent. We were not allowed to speak to anyone unless there was a good reason, such as confession. This took place weekly, normally at the same set time, and we confessed our sins to the elder. It was a strange and difficult situation when we had to tell him our negative thoughts, and especially when these concerned the elder himself. It was also something which relieved me of a feeling of guilt. It was another step along the path of deliberation and cleansing of my soul.

In the end, we retired to our cells, where we could read for an hour or two before sleep. This was my favorite part of the day. My mind travelled to other places and eras. Of course, I must point out that most of the books we read had theological, philosophical, or historical content, such as *The mental struggle*, stories of older monks and hermits, extra-biblical references to Jesus etc. We also had the full collection of *Migne's Patrologia Graeca*, 161 volumes of writings of Church Fathers, spanning from the early days till about the 11th century, and subsequently compiled in the mid-1800s. We also read a great deal about herbs and plants. I remember reading a whole book dedicated to garlic; half was comprised of historical references and legends and the other half, remedies and physical attributes. Near the end of my stay, I managed to get access to books of a broader scope. I'll expand more on these books in a later chapter.

- *All-night vigils*

About once a month we had a great gathering to celebrate a saint, a story of Jesus or the Virgin Mary, or the patron saint of a monastery that belonged to the same denomination as ours. On these days, we set out on foot to go to these hermitages a day earlier. Some of our visitors came with us. The hike lasted about two to three hours, and we reached our destination before sunset. If the chapel celebrated the patron saint, then we helped with the preparation of dinner. On such great celebrations, the meal usually consisted of fish and vegetables, and it was the only time that we could have an extra glass of wine. If the hermitage had its own visitors, and we added in our own, we comprised about thirty people. That was a large number for the small hermitages in our area, but we did not mind the inconvenience, because we enjoyed the extra company and the change in daily routine.

The fact that during these gatherings we got to know other people and have conversations gave us great joy. Living with other men twenty-four hours a day for 365 days a year in a confined space, such as our monastery, was something exceedingly difficult. We had to respect one another's faults, keeping a fine balance, but we had nothing to talk about. We had already talked about everything; we knew everyone else's views on every subject, and any attempt to discuss things was a boring repetition of the same themes. Therefore, being in contact with people we had never seen before was a bright outlet. An opportunity for novel discussions, to be exposed to new points of view and ideas.

After dinner, vigilance began. Vigilances are part of the ancient tradition of the church and give the service a special meditative character. We all contributed to the service in the order that the *Typikaris* (the monk responsible for the order of the ritual) determined. The roles that were appointed were: a right, or main chanter, and a helper. The left chanter or *Labadarios* and his helper, the *Kanonarhis*, who dictated to the chanters which melody to chant; there was the caretaker of the church, who lit and extinguished the candles in order, depending on the stage of the service. He also burnt incense and had other similar duties. The rest of the monks read in turn, for about fifteen minutes each. Everything was done ritually. Each time the *Kanonarhis* finished dictating, he bowed towards the chanters. By doing so, he was asking for their forgiveness regarding whether he had pronounced something incorrectly, whether he had not spoken clearly, or whether he had started dictating before the chanter had finished.

Vigilance lasted about ten to fourteen hours, with the congregation standing up most of the time. So, it made sense that some people could not endure it in its entirety and went to get some rest, especially during the readings of the Service of the Hours, right before the *Liturgy* started. Some others sat for a while on the church stalls to rest, and they often dozed off, but someone always woke them up.

During the vigilance, and especially before Holy Communion, we were encouraged to recall feelings of devastation. We thought about the bad thoughts we had had, our sins, our misbehaviors towards others, and we took notice of them in order not to repeat them. We felt like sinners, unable to receive the Body and Blood of Christ inside us. We had to cleanse our hearts at all costs, even at the last minute before we received Holy Communion. If someone was terribly remorseful about a deed or thought of his, he felt a lump in his throat approaching the Holy Grail. We had heard stories about monks who choked on the Holy Communion because they did not have a clean heart. The faith of a believer transforms what he receives into what he believes. The power of believing is immense.

After the end of the night service, we would have a meal. Normally, we would call it breakfast since the sun was already up, but it resembled dinner, since we had fish, octopus, or squid with salad and cheese, wine, and fruit! The worst situation to be in was if you had been chosen to read out the story of the day being celebrated while the others were eating. Being up all night, chanting and serving, gave you a big appetite, and then you would have to wait another hour before you could eat, all while smelling the food and listening to others eat. Somebody had to do that, and it was usually done voluntarily by our *Typikaris*. He was the best monk, willing and obedient.

In the end, we were served coffee, and it was the last chance to talk with the other monks and visitors. We would see the monks again in about a month and the visitors perhaps in a year, or most likely never again.

When we returned to our cells, we went to bed, using dark shades in the cell. I remember that when we laid down, we had a feeling of contentment because we had managed to carry out the vigilance. Moreover, we had no duties on that day, which meant we had ample time to get a good book, sit under a tree, and read while listening to nature. The simplest things in life filled us with joy and gratitude, probably because we voluntarily deprived ourselves of many other pleasures.

- *Hygiene*

Another great concern was personal cleanliness and hygiene. The cleanliness of each monk was different from place to place, but everywhere it was below the normal level. In our brotherhood there was not even a shower. I had to insist on the need for a tap in one of the toilets so that we could wash our sensitive parts. We washed our heads once every two to three months. Some, like myself, did not even use shampoo, just cold water. On top of that, some did not even brush their teeth or wash their face.

The result of these practices was that the whole house had an odor that visitors detected immediately. However, we had gotten used to it. I do believe that there are some limits to the odor the body emits. Some of us washed our clothes, which reduced the odor. Of course, incense was also helpful because it acted as cologne. The fact that we never ate meat also changed the smell of our bodies, making it less heavy. Of course, those of you who have actually visited a hermitage will know that these considerations could ameliorate the situation only so much.

The reasons behind this limited personal hygiene are, of course, spiritual. The first reason is that a monk must not see his body naked, to avoid memories and thoughts of bodily pleasures. The second reason is that the monk is cut off from society to take care of his soul and not his body. We were there to raise our spirit through prayer and communion with the divine, not to be attractive to the rest of the world. Ultimately, we wanted to save our soul because it had divine grace and would receive God's eternal blessing.

The only place which was relatively clean was the kitchen. When we had no food cooked in oil, we rinsed the plates only with water to save on dishwashing liquid. The cast iron oven was always black and sticky to the touch. I remember one time when a father and his son who had come to visit entered the dining room to eat. The son asked his father to leave to avoid getting food poisoning. I do not blame them; they had their point. We were apparently immune.

Had we gotten used to the primitive hygiene or was it a matter of faith as well? I do not know. I also do not know how we avoided getting sick from the water we drank. In the summer, we had running water straight from the spring. Sometimes we found small dead animals, or even just skeletons, in the little cistern that collected the spring water before it went into the pipes. In the winter, we had water from a big cement tank, in which we always found spiders and insects. The hand water pump was incredibly old and completely rusty.

I know many visitors who got ill because of our water. It was not harmful to us though. I met elderly monks who had lived on Athos for fifty to sixty years and were harmed by nothing. Apparently, our immune system had adapted to this way of life. At the beginning of my monastic life, I remember having some abdominal problems.

Our faith on this issue was a denial of truth. It may have been this denial which helped us survive and not get poisoned. Because with faith comes a lack of fear. And fear cripples the body and the soul. Perhaps the bottom line is that everything exists in our mind. Or as Paul put it in Hebrews 11:1, "*faith is the substance of things hoped for.*" Believing is just so powerful!

Image 20 – The author collecting herbs for dinner. The taste of those herbs was remarkable.

Chapter 6. The cook

If I have a faith that can move mountains,
but do not have love, I am nothing.
1 Corinthians 13:2

It is tradition that, when the elder of a brotherhood passes away, the next in hierarchy takes his place. The hierarchy is established by the time one enters a rank. So, the first rank is composed of the monks of the Great Schema, i.e., the ones who took the oath. Next come the *rasoefhi* monks, those who had received a blessing without taking any oaths, and finally the novices. Everyone has a rank, which is reflected in where you sit to eat or when you get in line for a ceremony, but it is not very important in everyday life. People with more skills eventually gain more control, even if they are in a lower rank.

When the old elder and founder of the brotherhood passed away in 1992, the cook was the highest in rank, but he declined to become the elder. He excused himself by saying that he was illiterate and would be of more service to the brotherhood holding his current positions, i.e., being the gardener and the cook. So, the priest became the elder, until about 2005, when he was summoned to another position, outside the mountain. Again, the cook refused to accept his rightful place as leader of the brotherhood, staying in the second place and allowing the third in hierarchy to become the elder, my elder.

The cook was born in 1926, so he was already eighty when I entered the monastery. He had a long, snow-white beard, long white hair fringing a big bald center, and he was very thin, almost skin and bones. He had been a goat shepherd as a young man and became a monk very young, in his early twenties. To that end, he did not receive much conventional education. However, he taught himself during all those years, and he could read and understand ancient scriptures adequately. Still, he was very blunt, abrasive, and could seem offensive to anyone that did not know him better. When he was teaching me gardening, he often expressed shock at my lack of knowledge, saying that I knew nothing besides eating and sleeping. I later realized that he was trying to help me control my pride and humble myself. But at first, I struggled not to lash out at him, since my ego was loudly proclaiming that I was an educated, strong, and healthy young man.

Image 21 - The sloped terrain was formed into layers with rock walls to allow for gardening.

This old and unpleasant man was, however, an example of love and self-sacrifice. He was totally motivated to serve the brotherhood. Because he was extremely intolerant of the midday heat, he did not rest after service but started working the gardens. In summer, we produced tomatoes, cucumbers, potatoes, eggplant, okra, peppers, artichokes, squash, onions, garlic, melons, watermelons, string beans and broad beans. In winter we produced carrots, spinach, lettuce, cabbage, broccoli, and cauliflower. We also had some trees: orange, lemon, apple, pear, pomegranate, apricot, and plum, some vineyards, and a lot of olive trees. The cook was responsible for all the plants but had help from the younger monks. Even in his mid-eighties, it was common to see him climbing a tree to trim it or pick its fruit. At the same time, he was the cook, so he was responsible for always having a hot plate in front of everyone when it was time to eat.

All this stress took a toll on his body, and he developed a severe skin reaction, especially in the summer, when his legs itched, and he scratched them until they bled. It was a pitiful scene, but he refused to relinquish his responsibilities. We all offered to step up and fill his role, but he refused again. He said that serving the brotherhood was his life, the only reason he kept going in his old age. In addition, he said that he loved the brotherhood more than himself, and he was ready to die while serving us.

He would tell us that hatred is like a virus in the heart that consumes you internally, but love heals everything. Hatred does not hurt the person who is hated, it hurts the person who hates. In addition, he told us that we could express love in many ways, even in a monastery. We could put off our work or sacrifice the little spare time to talk to someone who needed a human touch, an ear to hear them. It is love for the fellow human that makes a monk open his house to any stranger who knocks on his door and feed him, to give him a bed to sleep in, and to talk to him. Bottom line: it was pure love, given without expecting a return.

In larger society, where there is more taking than giving, such unconditional love is not common. However, even if we cannot love everyone, we can at least stop being indifferent. It can start with the smallest things, like smiling at someone or holding the door. There is also giving to those in need. Giving can be time, effort, money, materials, words, prayers, positive thoughts, advice, visits, anything. If it is done with a clean heart and good intentions, you are rewarded with feelings of happiness and fulfillment.

Chapter 7. The teacher

Victory over self is of all victories the first and best,
while self-defeat is of all defeats at once
the worst and the most shameful.
Plato, Laws, 626e

Another person worth describing was my iconography teacher. He had also been a goat shepherd who grew up in a very small village in the mountains of northwest Greece, where the snow melted for only four to five months every year. When he was about twenty, he moved to a nearby city and learned the trade of making fur clothes. He was not satisfied with his life but also did not know what to do, so he went to Mount Athos in search of answers. He visited a famous hermit named Paisios, who calmed him saying: "Do not worry, we do not force people to stay here." It was as though Paisios had read his mind and knew that he was considering becoming a monk. As he was leaving, the old hermit told him: "Tell your brother's partner Mr. X to leave the business to both of you. It will be fine." My teacher was shocked, as he claims he did not mention Mr. X or his business endeavors to the hermit. That event made him decide to become a monk. And he became a monk with such fervor and zeal that he became the strictest monk that I met. But he was strict only towards himself, not others.

Everything my iconography teacher did was very disciplined. He never sat down during church service, whether it was a thirty-minute service or a fourteen-hour all-night vigil. On those occasions, he would doze off while standing and would wake up as he was falling. He never ate or slept too much, and he did not wash his face on a daily basis. On top of the regular restrictions that he placed on his life, which were in addition to the already harsh monastic life, he would challenge himself from time to time. Once, he did not speak for forty days. He avoided any conversation, and if we pressed him, he only nodded or mumbled a *yes* or *no*. Finally, we realized what he was doing and tried to accommodate him, but it was annoying, especially if there was some information we needed from him.

Sometimes the iconography teacher would not eat or drink water. He would still come and sit in his place, with the food served in front of him, but he would not take a bite. Other times he ate very little, e.g., taking only three sips of his soup. On some occasions, he didn't even sleep. As my cell was adjacent to a huge rock where he would hang out when his cell was hot, I could hear his noises in the silence of the night. Once, I went to wake him up for the midnight service, his door was open, and I saw him asleep, kneeling by his bed. Sometimes he stayed out all night in the winter to freeze himself. You could tell by the color of his face.

He also vowed never to talk on the phone. Sometimes his relatives would call and ask about him. Whoever answered the phone would tell them the news of his health and convey his greetings. He also hated technology and did not even own a flashlight, only a gas lamp. The most advanced technology he used was a clock.

Although the iconography teacher read a great deal, he never tried to teach anyone, either visitors or novice monks. He tried to keep to himself and tried to remain quiet as much as possible. Only if you asked him a direct question would he answer, and then very directly and without elaboration. He was very obedient to the elders. Although he was the third in the hierarchy, he would gladly perform anything that he was asked, even if he was hungry, thirsty, sleepy, or sick. He was the perfect monk; any elder would like to have him as a subordinate.

Even though he did not teach with words, he taught by his example. And, although his actions were extreme, and I worried about his health, I realized that true discipline develops very slowly, in increments, through repetition. It might be forcing yourself to wake up after three hours of sleep or not eating when you were hungry. It might entail not bursting out in anger when you wanted to. Or it might comprise reading or doing something you don't want to do. Discipline is the power that the mind exercises over the body, the control the inner self exerts on the outer self.

One of the best ways to build discipline is through fasting. I learned this by observing my iconography teacher. Fasting can take the form of abstaining from all food for short periods of time, or from fats and animal products for extended periods. I am not a medical expert, so I will not expound on the benefits fasting has on the body, which I believe are many. But I will mention the benefits I found that it has on the mind and on life in general.

Fasting bolsters clarity of mind and reduces apathy and lethargy. I must admit that there is a certain threshold at which the benefits start to become visible, because until the body gets used to fasting, it fights back. A strong will and discipline are necessary to fast, which conditions your mind to become more disciplined. For example, if you decide not to eat a specific favorite food, or to give up eating entirely for a time, and you happen to be around that food, there is going to be a battle raging in your head. The body is hungry and wants to eat, signaling its desires to the brain. Thoughts arise as to why you should break your fast and enjoy the food. Your higher self will have to suppress that thinking and remain firm. This process strengthens your mind and trains it for making future decisions that are much tougher.

I will share another story to prove this point. One day I decided to do sit-ups daily, without missing a day for any reason. After a while, my body got used to the original number of repetitions and I decided to add ten every day. I never skipped a day of doing this workout and always added ten each day. After a while I reached 500 continuous sit-ups, which took about forty-five minutes to complete. The body just obeys a disciplined mind.

Chapter 8. The annual celebration of Lavra

He who serves the most, reaps the most.

Jim Rohn

All property on Mount Athos belongs to the twenty big monasteries. Each of the hundreds of sketes, cabins, huts, caves, or dwellings that are spread all over the peninsula belongs to one of the twenty monasteries and must obtain permission for building or developing the land. It is also implied that the elder of each brotherhood (or the sole inhabitant of a hut), accepts the ecclesiastical authority of the elder of the big monastery, to which the land belongs. When an elder wants to ordain a monk, the big monastery must be informed. At that point, the monk surrenders his identification card from the state and receives a new card, with his new monk's name. This card is also accepted by Greek authorities.

Being in a brotherhood of radicals or *zealots*, we did not recognize the authority of the monastery to which we belonged, the Great Lavra Monastery. We did not bow down and kiss their elders' hands, nor did we hold prayer with them. In response, they refused to approve any new ordinations, which meant that after the death of the last old ones, accepted forty years before, there would be no legal successor, and we could potentially be evicted from the property. Even though the newer monks of our brotherhood took the oaths and went through all the ceremonies, their legal status was still civilian.

That was by itself a heavy burden on our hearts. There was a feeling that we were guests in our home, that we should not get overly attached to earthly belongings, even more so than the usual monk should not be. We had contingency plans, such as moving to another monastery near a city, and having a bag packed with the necessary materials, ready for flight, if needed. Fortunately, we did not have that problem, though I know of some other radicals from our greater neighborhood who were evicted, not necessarily solely because of their ideology, but because of their conduct and behavior in general. Behaviors that could be pardoned in other cases, such as growing marijuana, were prosecuted to the maximum extent with *zealots*, usually resulting in eviction.

There was only one obligation to the Great Lavra Monastery that we upheld: our service to the annual celebration of St. Athanasios of Athos, who built the monastery in 963 AD. Every year, more than 300 people gather on July the 18th to commemorate the passing of the founder. The celebration lasted four days, and the preparations were a huge burden for the monks of the Great Lavra, as on top of their everyday chores and attendance to the lengthy services, they had to feed and sleep 300 extra people, twice a day. For that, they summoned the help of monks that lived outside the monastery, on one of the monastery's properties, and gave them a responsibility.

Our brotherhood's responsibility was to serve water, wine, bread, cheese, and dessert. Every year, three or four brothers would travel via boat to the Great Lavra monastery and stay there for four days. There were two days of preparation for the main event and one day following it. In the dining hall, there were about twenty-four marble tables. The marble of the tables and benches was centuries old, probably from the 10th century, which was evident from the holes and erosion. In the past, when the monastery was understaffed, the ceiling leaked, and the drip of water resulted in holes in the marble over the years. So, we had to be careful where to place the cups so they would not topple over. We also had to be very fast because most of the times the dining hall was not large enough for all the guests and hosting monks, so after the first batch was finished eating, we had to clean up and set up for the second. Sometimes there would be a third batch. Our main responsibilities were to cut the cheese into servings and slice the loaves of bread right before each meal so that it would not dry out. Wine was poured in pitchers from the barrels that we had to carry from the cellar, but in the exact amount. This was to avoid the wine going sour. Water was poured into pitchers right before dining time, so it would still be cool. Lastly, the dessert was taken out of the fridge and placed on the tables. When the bell rang, almost 300 hungry people would walk into the hall, and we facilitated the seating. Each table had to be filled to its maximum capacity. After prayer, people started eating, and we would rush around, filling up water pitchers or bread trays or accommodating whatever needs the diners might have.

Image 22 - Holes on the 1000-year-old marble table from decades of water dripping on it. There were larger holes than the ones depicted here.

After everyone had finished eating, it was our turn to eat. It was one of those times where we could indulge in some extra food, like extra cheese or extra dessert. We even had a glass of wine every day, even if it was a weekday. We then prepared for the next meal through tasks such as bringing a hundred loaves of bread in from the bakery, or a couple barrels of wine from the cellar. Then we would retire to our rooms, exhausted but happy.

There is something about serving, especially feeding somebody who is hungry, that is very fulfilling. By hungry, I do not mean hungry because of poverty, just when you serve someone that is hungry. And they were hungry, after a fourteen-hour all-night vigil or a day full of ceremonies and litanies. This was especially true of civilians used to three or more meals a day, who found it difficult to eat only twice a day. The last day, before everybody departed, there was not a second serving in the dining hall. Only the people that fit in the hall ate there, and the rest were served on plastic plates and ate outside, after which they took their leave. That was when I felt the most gratitude from the people, and the most satisfaction in my heart. Giving the food directly from your hands to theirs, hearing them express their gratitude and thankfulness, fulfilling their requests for more bread or second portions, had an exhilarating effect. All the tiredness, the mosquito bites, the sweaty restless nights in the hot rooms they would provide for us, were forgotten at that moment, and the decision to do it again next year or somewhere else was made.

This annual service has made me realize that serving your fellow human is a very profitable path in life. Once we find out what we are good at, or what we like doing, we can think of ways to use that to serve people around us. Not only do we keep doing what we like, and become better at it, but we also help people around us, contributing to society. For example, if someone likes drawing, a way to serve is to offer lessons to young or troubled people. Not only do they become better at drawing by teaching it, but they also help the students to acquire a skill or find a passion.

In the monastic world, there is a path named "the calling after perfection," where a monk who has reached the state of *apathia* or becomes "perfect," might receive a calling to serve society in a number of ways. There are old stories of monks that felt this calling and returned to society, in the midst of temptations that would not affect them anymore, to heal wounds in leprosy outbreaks, to feed homeless people, or to start a hospice and take in elderly people. In our days, I knew of monks who may or may not have been "perfect," but were still susceptible to temptations. Nevertheless, they travelled the country holding meetings with people that needed some guidance. The difference in such service might be in the motivation: it might be purely to serve fellow humans, or it might reflect an inability to stay enclosed in their monasteries, as they had vowed to do.

Image 23 – The dining hall of Great Lavra monastery.

Chapter 9. Dissent

A fanatic is one who can't change his mind
and won't change the subject.

Winston Churchill

When I entered the monastery, our church faced a serious problem that had divided its followers. There were two icons that depicted the Holy Trinity, one from the 5th century AD, the other from the 10th century AD. The first group contended that we had to keep only the first icon, as it was the oldest and depicted a theme from the Old Testament, while the second group supported keeping only the second icon. Naturally, as often happens in cases of great dissent, there could be a compromise. In this case, it was the church council that said we should keep both icons to avoid a *schism* (division) within the church, somehow allowing both views to coexist.

Image 24 - The icon from the 5th century AD.

Image 25 - The icon from the 10th century AD.

This controversy permeated the whole monastery, dividing the monks as well. When I arrived, I found them divided into two rival camps. They all agreed that both icons were acceptable. But some, like my elder and most other monks, were intolerant of different views. Just as they were rigid about commemorating the Ecumenical Patriarch, the stance towards the people who did so, and the use of technology, in that vein, they also refused to accept a new rule that emphasized the importance of one icon over the other. They wanted to sever relations with the church council and everyone who had an opinion different than theirs on the matter. In the other camp was the priest, who had taken a middle-of-the-road stance and agreed with the council, and the cook, who happened to be the eldest of all. As soon as I arrived, I had to choose a side. My elder was not fond of the priest, but the priest was closer to me. Besides, it was he who had greatly influenced my decision to become a monk.

This was not the best environment for a new monk. When I went there, I expected to find Jesus's love amongst the monks. Instead of that, I found tense relations, seemingly ready to sunder the brotherhood. The priest had warned me that something odd was happening between my elder and the other monks, but I did not expect all this. As soon as I arrived, the elder tried to draw me to his side and cut me off from the priest. Instead of reading prayer books, they had me read about holy icons, symbolism, and how those symbols were established in the church of the 9th century A.D. They pressured me to go along with their position, and made it clear in their own indirect way that if I did not agree with their ideas, I would not be welcome in the brotherhood.

However, I felt totally indifferent to this issue, so I tried to gain time until the priest returned. I wanted to hear his stand on the issue. When he returned, we discussed the issue:
- The elder and the brothers say that you don't accept Abraham's Hospitality as an icon of the Holy Trinity.
- I accept both icons.
- But you signed the document that condemns it.
- It doesn't condemn the old icon, just sets the new as preferred. It was a maneuver to keep the hotheaded of the other side from separating, we will fix it in the next encyclical document.
- But the *others* consider it heresy to accept the old icon. The brotherhood can't stay in communication with them.
- Let's try to give them some time to understand and when spirits have calmed down, we can fix it.

Thus, I realized that his views were much more neutral and that the only thing he wanted was to avoid a schism. None of the things he was accused of were true. Past grievances and personal issues had clouded the brotherhood's judgment and they were looking for a reason to ostracize the priest. In other words, other issues, possibly power games within the Church council, were the reason for the dissent in the first place, and the icons served merely as a pretext for all this.

That was a period of fanaticism and irrationality. Diatribes were cast against prominent members of each side. Families were divided and went to different churches, many miles apart. Monks and nuns were forced out of their monasteries. Priests shifted alliances with the promise of a promotion. Punishable acts from clerics were swept under the rug in exchange for support on the conflict. The team to which my elder belonged was so fanatical that they decided to break away from the council, if it kept maintaining its middle-of-the-road stance.

After the priest returned, a party of the "neutrals" was organized. Having the cook on that side made it safe for me to join the neutral team. The cook, as the oldest, had everyone's respect, including that of my elder. Of course, I never openly disagreed with my elder. I maintained a middle ground and tried to reconcile both teams. Besides, I was not particularly interested in the issue, and thinking back, I understand how meaningless all these disputes were.

Over time, however, the priest and I started to have some disagreements, largely about everyday issues not related to the two icons. Most of the issues were work related. As an example, I would help him produce wooden crosses. He was very detail-oriented, and I was more production-oriented, as he was always behind on orders. He pressed me to pay more attention to superfluous details. When I was painting a wall, he also impelled me to drain the mixing stick thoroughly, wasting more time, which was disproportionate to the value of the paint saved. This was extremely annoying, as you might imagine. That is why I decided to follow the team of my elder and get away from the priest to find peace. It was then that I comprehended I was not the only one who changed teams for personal reasons. I also understood that prejudice and fanaticism affected nearly everyone's judgement.

While being on the priest's team, I read an old text which seemed to confirm his views, but when I went to my elder's team and read the same text again, my mind interpreted it in a different way that justified my elder's points of view. The text was a writing of St. John of Damascus, dealing with the three men that visited Abraham and their identities. This need for self-justification in deciding to change teams made me see things differently. Reflecting on this later, I realized that we should be humble and never too fanatical with our opinions. Even when you think you are open-minded and just analyzing the facts, your biases and prejudice might be embedded on a level deeper than you can attain at the moment, distorting your analysis.

Fortunately for me, I never took the issue with the icons too seriously and so avoided taking extreme positions. The situation never developed into open conflict, and, in time, the issue started to fade. Yet, after conflict, residues usually remain, shadows which mar relationships. This was the case of my elder and the priest. Their relations were never healthy again.

This issue of dissent lasted for years, and through all these examples of fanaticism I experienced, I realized that I should never trust those who claim to hold the absolute truth. Truth is subjective to everyone - in the sense that as humans we are unable to grasp the absolute truth - and reality seems to change for everyone depending on one's perspective.

Image 26 – A good fishing day included moray-eels and rockfish.

Chapter 10. The problem of fishing and the solution of solar panels

A faith is a necessity to a man.
Woe to him who believes in nothing.
Victor Hugo

About a year before I entered the monastery, another person came to the brotherhood as a novice. This brother had a passion for fishing and received the elder's permission to go fishing once a week with the boat. One time I asked to go with him, and the elder gladly gave me his blessing. In this way he believed he would draw me to his side and keep me away from the priest, who had greater influence on me.

Image 27 - The little dingy we used to fish the sea around Karoulia.

Thus, we started to fish once a week, weather permitting. The priest, however, was very strict about this issue. He did not want us to fish. He insisted, and told the elder, that because of the short time we had been on Athos, fishing would be an activity that would distract our minds and hearts from the sacred duty of a monk, which is to keep his attention focused on his soul. He said that outside the brotherhood, we would talk a great deal, talk about petty things and laugh, both of which were forbidden in monasticism. On the other hand, the elder retorted that we should be able to let off steam occasionally. He would tell the story of Saint Antonios (the 3rd century hermit monk) and the hunter. A hunter was scandalized when he saw Antonios having fun with the other brothers. Antonios wanted to teach the hunter, so he said: "Put an arrow on your bow and stretch it," which he did. Then Antonios said: "Stretch it some more," which he did. Antonios then told him again: "Stretch it even more." The hunter replied: "If I stretch it too much, the bow will break." And Antonios said to him placidly: "The same thing happens with our monastic life. If we are extreme with our behavior towards our brothers, they will also break. Therefore, we should sometimes be considerate to them and their needs."

All this story with the fishing resulted in a great conflict between the elder and the priest, the latter of whom took it to the point of not eating any of our fish, as a way to protest. However, the priest himself had his way to unwind; every so often he left the Holy Mount and went to different places to carry out church services. He also had his tools and machines, which comprised his hobby. In particular, he had welding machines, lawn mowers, drills, a power generator, and various other things. All this was too advanced for life in a hermitage, and it had been a cause of past dissent in the brotherhood involving a previous elder. This was a conflict which lasted many years. However, everyone needed and should have some way to unwind. Ours was fishing.

Image 28 - Cooking the fish we caught.

After some time, another brother stopped eating our fish. He also thought that it was unreasonable for two novice monks to stay away from the monastery the whole day that often. This was a problem for the cook, because we all ate together, but as he was fond of us as well as the fish, he said nothing, exercising patience.

The priest lived in a building just outside the brotherhood. He had solar panels installed to provide electricity for his machines and power tools. The elder feared that the priest would leave the brotherhood and stay with the council. That meant that we would no longer have contact with him. When the elder saw that I no longer got along with the priest, he told me that he had a plan for us to get our own electricity. So, he assigned me the task of doing research, in order to buy and install solar panels. We had already bought two deep freezers and a refrigerator, but the priest's panels could not support their demand for electricity. That justified starting our own energy production. It was obvious that the elder did not want to have much contact with the priest or rely on him for our energy. First, we found a place to build a storehouse for the batteries and the other equipment. We were going to place the panels on top of the storehouse. However, in order to build the storehouse in the place we had found, we had to uproot an old leftover stump of a huge olive tree. It took three of us three days just to dig out its very deep roots.

The second stage was to build the storehouse, so we hired two people to help us. The logistics of acquiring all the necessary materials was a nightmare. Everything was carried from the port to the hermitage on mules, many times in adverse weather. I remember one time we had ordered a truck full of gravel and iron bars, and before we had finished taking them out of the ship a storm arose. Another brother and I shoveled the gravel away from the dock and moved it several feet up the shore. But before we had secured the iron bars, the waves washed out all the gravel. Greatly disappointed, we went up to the hermitage. However, the other brother, seeing the waves going over the dock, worried about the iron bars and decided to go back. I tried to make him change his mind and said that it was not worth risking his life for some iron bars, but he would not listen. I was proved right because he had an accident. What saved his life was that he took someone along to help him. As he was on top of a building about fifteen feet above sea level, a big wave hit him and knocked him unconscious. Fortunately, the other person was there and caught him just before he was literally swallowed by the sea.

After quite a few other problems, construction began. Whenever we had to make a layer of concrete, many from the neighborhood came to help. This was something common, but nevertheless great. When there was someone in need in the neighborhood, we all helped. In the Athos language this is called "*pankinia.*"

Being autonomous for energy and not relying on the priest was liberating. But the problem was finally resolved when the priest left the brotherhood for good and become a bishop in a city.

This story exemplifies the value of patience. The cook had every right to prepare only the fish, forcing the dissenting monks to eat or starve. He also had the right to not cook our fish, because not everyone wanted them. Instead, he chose to burden himself with cooking two meals each time, keeping both sides in balance.

Exercising unlimited patience was particularly important in the monastic community. When some monks were asked: "How are you doing?" they would reply: "Just being patient," almost like a mantra. There were stories of people who were abused for years and just kept being patient instead of revolting. They were trying to adapt their inner state rather than alter the circumstances that caused the situation.

Image 29 – The feeling of freedom in the wilderness was indescribable. Even my hair was set free from the mandatory cap.

Chapter 11. Untamed?

There is a very fine line between loving life and being greedy for it.

Maya Angelou

When a visitor comes to Mount Athos for the first time, the first thing he notices is the harmony between nature and man-made monasteries. The next things that impress them are the feeling of reverence inside the temples and around them, as well as the harmony and placidity in the monks' interpersonal relations. The latter is the most difficult to achieve. Many people consider continuous fasting, sleep deprivation, or even the lack of satiation of some bodily needs, such as sex, the most difficult things in monastic life. No matter how paradoxical this sounds, these are the easy parts of monasticism. It was somehow difficult, especially in the beginning, but it could not compare to the unconditional surrender of your will to your elder spiritual father. When you enter a monastery to become a monk, you abandon your ego from the outside world. You declare absolute submission to your elder. On top of all this, you are not to maintain a point of view about any matters whatsoever. Everything is up to the elder, and the rest have no other responsibility but to execute his orders. There are stories about monks who accomplished this, and as a result they managed to reach a level of deep inner peace. Because they did not have any responsibility for what happened around them, they could focus on improving their souls, as their elder was responsible for everything else.

However, our ego is a giant within us, whom we nurture from childhood. Is it possible to uproot it suddenly? How can we stand our own humiliation? It might seem like a Herculean task! Still, I have known monks who managed to do this. They were educated people, extremely subservient to their elder, even if he was an uneducated old man. In other cases, they may have been uneducated people in search of their soul, seekers of truth who longed for inner peace, tired, and frustrated by the wickedness of man and society.

Nevertheless, some cannot bear the annihilation of ego and obedience to orders. On the one hand, they seek tranquility and strengthening of their soul, but they cannot accept everything. Most of them leave the hermitages to which they had originally been assigned and go to live alone without needing to be spiritually or psychologically in accord with monastic principles. We called them "*thelimatarides*," i.e. untamed, hard-headed, because they followed their own will and stubbornness. In Athos parlance, there is an old saying that those men could build something as high as the peak of Athos.

We also had an old monk who had lived in our brotherhood for many years. He was ill and could not contribute much to the brotherhood. At one moment, he decided to leave and live on his own. He found a deserted hut, about a five-minute walk from us. There, he not only recovered from illness but made the hut livable and cleared the stones from all the paths leading to his home. This happened because he wanted to do it himself, being forced by no one. At last, he was alone and happy.

In my case, I did not believe that I could be all alone. I considered myself unprepared, not physically, but spiritually. I needed a guide for my spiritual ascent, but it was difficult for me to blindly follow my elder's orders. Surrendering my will to another man was not an easy matter for me at all. On the other hand, I did not have a problem with the elder, because he was a kind, good-hearted old man. After the priest had left, our relations were particularly good. I worked hard at what he asked, and he allowed me to do certain things separately from the others. Of course, I did not ask for extravagant things, as I did not want to put him in a tough spot. Besides, I had enough freedom compared to others.

The truth is, I did certain things secretly from him and the other monks. I was sure that if I had asked for his permission, he would not have given it to me. I had to do these things, though, because they helped me unwind and break free. I could not be physically inactive and just pray. There was so much energy inside me, and I had to channel it somewhere. So, whenever I had free time, I sneaked into the storehouse and worked. Everybody knew that I made walking sticks, but this was just a distraction in case somebody walked in. In fact, to pass the time I made bows and arrows. I made bows from oak, bamboo, and even metal. In addition, I shot some arrows in the barn, using hay bales as targets, which was fun.

After the ordinary bows, I made a crossbow. It took me a week, at the expense of my duties, to make it. When I took my first shot, the crossbow broke, because I had used a steel cable as a string. I needed a real bow string, with elasticity, and I had to find the money to buy it. It was the first time, in five years, that I needed money. Of course, I could not ask for the funds from my elder, because then I would have to reveal the reason that I wanted them. Suffice it to say, he would not only have refused to give it to me, but he would have forbidden me to do things that did not help my soul, and I would have had to obey. I always obeyed all his direct orders until the day I left. He would not have been able to understand that these tasks helped uplift my soul or even keep my sanity. I had to manage some part of my life independently. I was and remain a practical man, not a theorist.

I had many tools at my disposal in the storehouse. Nobody used them after the priest's departure. That is why I decided to make various things out of materials I found in nature and give them to friends who visited me, so they would sell them on my behalf. I had made little wooden candlestick holders in different shapes, lighters and pen cases out of snakeskin, even leather wallets out of moray-eel skin. So, my friends from outside the mountain sold what I gave them and bought me what I needed.

Image 30 - My crossbow.

During that period, a friend gave me a laptop. We had just bought a laptop for a monk who studied some documents, and so I managed to keep my laptop unnoticed. My elder never realized that my own laptop was not the one he had approved. He believed the one inside the hermitage was the only one.

Then, another friend gave me another idea: to start an e-shop and promote the products I made through it. He was going to undertake the web page creation and the promotion of the products.

The business went very well. I told everyone that it was a friend's business. The monks of our brotherhood and the neighbors were interested in selling their hand-made things through this web page. Now, we also made a profit from the sale of other products. Because the brotherhood always had packages to send, I also sneaked in some of mine with the bulk.

The next obvious step was to get an Internet connection. I had installed a small solar panel on the roof of the house to power the two-way radio we had to communicate with neighbors. That solar panel happened to be above my cell. So, I asked a friend from college who was coming to visit to bring a broadband transmitter and the longest USB cable extension he could find. I used a special elastic tape to waterproof the transmitter that was connected to the end of the USB cable and placed it under the solar panel on the roof. The other end of the USB cable, which I believe was 6 meters long, was barely long enough to reach my laptop when I placed it on the windowsill. The Internet speed was fantastic, considering I was probably the only web-based user of the local cell tower! If anyone asked about that cable, I was prepared to answer that it was to monitor the solar panel's energy output. Now, think about it. Inside a *zealot's* cell, where trade was prohibited for the monks, with no electricity and only gas lamps by which to read, I had Internet! I guess I should have left earlier!

My next step was to create a small orchid plant. From the moment I started making things, I could in no way stop. But this project was too major in scope, and I could not keep it secret. Therefore, I asked my elder's permission and blessing, which he of course refused. The truth is that this refusal saddened me because I had learned to do what I wanted secretly, but it also taught me something. As a result, I became aware that occasionally the elder needed to deny his monks' requests to show them who was in charge. It also showed to me how much I had deviated from the monk's path: a monk does not get sad when denied a request because he has no will of his own.

But I could not accept the elder's refusal; it brought my egotism to the surface. To that end, I could not remain inactive. I had to do something. Therefore, I decided to grow the so-called super fruits, such as goji berries, sea-buckthorn, blueberries, and so on. I was sure that the elder could not refuse, because the diet of the monks was poor in vitamins. That would be something useful for the brotherhood, a means of promoting general health. Despite my certainty about it, however, I started in secret again. Apparently, I had become addicted to the adrenaline that came from secret and illicit deeds designed to circumvent the rules of the brotherhood.

I planted a goji berry seed in a small bowl and left it outside my window. When it grew a little, I replanted it somewhere outside the cell. By the fall of the same year, it had already produced fruit. So, I took the fruit in my hand and went to speak to my elder. In this way, I managed to obtain his blessing and continue. That is how I started. I cleared all the stones, opened holes, put the plants in them, and fenced up the place so that animals would not eat the plants. I fitted hoses with sprinklers at the roots of the plants for watering and made a small greenhouse for the avocados.

All this hard work made me feel happy because it was something I wanted to do. My elder's permission did not matter. I believed that this plot of land belonged to me in some way. No one could come and tell me what to do. On this small piece of land, I was free. This plot of land was my world, my home. Of course, I knew nothing actually belongs to us, that we are passing through life, and all the things we believe we own will be left behind. Nevertheless, I felt happy with my life in that place. It was a period when I had the blessing to live without worrying about the future. The bottom line might be that happiness comes when we stop worrying about the future.

I also decided to make a small wooden bed under a tree, where I slept during the summer when it was extremely hot in my cell. It was made in such a way that worked as a Faraday cage. It was perfect to protect me from mosquitoes, but also from radio waves, which were already minimal up there. It worked; a cell phone had almost no signal when I closed the hatch. The experiment was a success!

Another thing that I constructed, and felt incredibly happy about, was a hut. I used it to get away from the routine of the monastery. I always got my elder's permission for day trips on Sundays or on other holidays when we didn't work. In this way, I was able to spend these hours building my hut. The place was roughly two hours away from the monastery and also twenty-five minutes off the main path, a fact that made it completely invisible to any passer-by.

Initially, I cut down some small trees, and I used the straightest of them for the three corners of the hut. For the fourth corner, I used the thick trunk of a fir tree, and from it I supported all the others. Then I thought about how to make the walls. I could think of only two ways. The first was to gather all the wood from the nearby area. The other was to use some tin sheets we had in the storeroom. I knew that this wasn't right, but to justify it, I told myself that I was not stealing them, but moving them to another place; they would still belong to the monastery.

The problem was how to take the tin sheets out of the storeroom without being noticed. I was very patient. One day my elder asked me to carry some materials to the springs, using the mules. The hut was on my way, and I had the chance to carry the tin sheets as well as transparent plastic sheets for the roof.

Image 31 - Carrying materials to build a hut on the mule Zarkos.

As soon as I had finished the hut, I made two wooden beds, one of them folding, to save space. I also needed a fireplace because the winter cold was unbearable. At one time, I told my little secret to a monk who was a good friend. He built the fireplace for me, using some big stones we found nearby, and cement mixed with dirt. To be exact, there was a huge pile of stones that seemed to have been made by a man, although I never learned the reason it was done. Probably someone else had built something there within the past 1000 years.

Image 32 - Building the fireplace for the hut.

I do not remember how I got permission from my elder to sleep outside, but I spent my first night in the hut with my monk friend and his dog. Everything was damp, and it was freezing. Smoke came out of the fireplace, and we had to leave the door open. My friend became ill after this experience, but I believe that it was worth it. The situation was dramatic, and we were inhaling smoke from the burning branches, but we were inside a hut I had made with my own hands. What I felt was great fulfillment. The only thing we heard was an owl sitting above us in a tree and some jackals howling in the night from a distance. I savored the tranquility.

Image 33 - On one of the tours around Athos, when I was alone and "free."

Image 34 – Halfway to the summit, wearing a sheep-wool cape.

Image 35 – A nice flat spot to spend the night, covered in a sheep-skin, during our Easter-time tours.

Chapter 12. Rigidity of dead bodies

Blessed are the dead, who die in the Lord.

Revelation 14:13

August 19th, 2010. I was in the forest, about 600 feet away from the monastery. The previous night we had had vigilance, and I was resting under an olive tree. There was a heat wave that day, but I was sleeping in the cool shade of the olive tree, in my mosquito-proof wooden bed. I thought I heard someone grunting, like labored breathing. However, I was so tired that I did not get up to investigate. Perhaps I thought that, if someone needed assistance, they would call and ask for help.

It was almost evening when I heard voices and a commotion, as if in a dream. At first, I did not take much notice of it, ignoring all the noise. I was at the transition point between sleep and awakening, a beautiful lethargic state, when I heard voices, closer, repeat: "We found him! We found him!" I jumped up, terrified, thinking that they were talking about me, and I ran towards them. They were carrying the lifeless body of an old monk of the brotherhood. They had found him dead in a clearing a few feet away from me, where he had also lain down to rest. He was eighty-three years old, and we surmised that his old heart had been unable to withstand the heat. They took him to his cell and put him on his bed.

I always have had some guilt in my heart. What if I had woken up when he was grunting? Could I have helped him? I will never find out, but at least I have learned a lesson for the future: help people that are in need, even if it is an inconvenience.

The normal procedure when a monk died at Mount Athos, or "rested," as they said, was to inform the police as a first step. There was a police station almost an hour's walk from the monastery. There were neither roads nor cars, and the police car was—a mule! If the monk was old, then the policeman did not call a coroner, but if there had been an accident or the deceased was young, a coroner's investigation was mandatory. If a monk died at night, then we had to wait until morning. As a result, the burial procedure usually commenced at least eight to ten hours after death.

After all the legal procedures had been dealt with, the ritual of burial started. We sewed the *raso*, the ceremonial black garment, around the dead body, then we covered the face with the *epanokalimafho* cloth and sewed them together. Then we left the dead body on a table, inside the church, for a few more hours. This way, the monks, or even the deceased's relatives from the outside world, had the chance to bid farewell to him. The rest of us monks read the book of Psalms for as many hours as the body remained there.

I remember sitting and looking at this old monk, realizing that just a few hours ago we had been talking together, and now he was gone. He used to tell us a story from the Nazi occupation of Greece. He was an eyewitness to an incident when he was thirteen or fourteen, and it had become deeply etched in his mind. Three men were to be hanged by the Nazis in retaliation for an act of resistance. They had caught two of the men responsible and decided to pick one more victim at random from the men of the village, to set an example. They picked a small, totally innocent old man. During the hanging of this old man, the rope broke twice. The crowd protested, shouting "innocent," but the indifferent Nazis tried a third time and finally managed to hang him.

The truth is that, for as long as I was standing next to his body, I was apprehensive. It was the first time I had been so close to a dead person by myself, and various silly thoughts crossed my mind, even though I had been taught, while I was on Mount Athos, and even by my mother, that people valued life on earth much more than they should. The thought of death should be with us both during sleep and wakefulness because the constant memory of death was the right tutor of both body and soul. The point, then, was not to think constantly about the time we'd die, but to accept that the moment of departure was decisive for eternity. The thought of death prevented us from doing unimportant things. As it is impossible for a hungry man not to have food on his mind, likewise it is impossible for someone interested in the salvation of his soul not to think of death. When I recalled these teachings, I ceased to fear or feel sorrow. Eventually, the only thing I prayed for was his soul's repose.

When the allotted time had passed, we took the body and went to bury it. We lowered the body into the grave in a sheet. Everything was so simple on Mount Athos. No coffins, no flowers, no tears, no sad faces. He was resting.

The strangest thing of all was that the old monk's body did not exhibit even the slightest sign of rigidity. After almost fifteen hours, his body was still soft and flexible. Even when we lowered him into his grave, his body was so flexible that he seemed merely to be sleeping. Normally, rigor mortis starts three to four hours after the moment of death and climaxes at twelve. At Mount Athos, this did not happen. I witnessed similar cases on three more occasions. I cannot explain how this happened, and in fact I never met anyone who could explain it to me. Almost everyone attributed it to the monks' diet, but I never met someone who could explain it more scientifically. There are many vegans who are not at Mount Athos who maintain a pure diet free of fats, meat, or animal products. However, from what I have heard, their bodies become rigid when they die.

In the monastery, the monks believed that this was a sign from God. We had also heard stories that this happened to some Buddhist monks who had managed to reach high levels of spirituality. Who knows? The role of faith is a mystery. We still do not comprehend everything that happens in our minds nor all the effects they have on our perception of reality. I truly do not know how what I witnessed happened. What I do know is that I saw it with my very own eyes and touched the bodies with my own hands. I leave it to your own judgement; perhaps it is a subject for further research.

Chapter 13. Exorcism

It is human nature to think wisely and to act in an absurd fashion.

Anatole France

When I first entered the monastery as a novice, there was a monk who everyone thought had been possessed by some evil spirit. Even he himself believed that. He was a very thin, tall man, in his mid-thirties, with eyes deep in their sockets. When he was in that state, possessed, he spoke with a strange voice, teasing everyone. He had a propensity for calling each one names, like "glasses", "goat shepherd", "fatso" and so on. Generally, he was harmless, but I learned that on the first day he became possessed, he grabbed a knife and threatened to kill everyone. He kicked a monk that tried to subdue him in the ribs, and it was painful for months after. Therefore, the monks were forced to perform an exorcism on him to bring him back to normalcy. When he spoke to me, he claimed that the evil spirit had possessed him. Once he was possessed, he could not control himself and heard a voice speaking to him.

I am neither a psychologist nor a psychiatrist. At that time, I was vulnerable, and believed him, although I had my reservations. One day something happened that strengthened my suspicions. I was in my cell studying when, suddenly, the door opened, and the tall monk jumped in and started shouting and mocking me, saying "You idiot, you have a college degree but locked yourself in a monastery!" I was startled, jumped up and instinctively pushed him out, but my shove was so violent that he nearly fell down the stairs and barely avoided injury. As he was falling backwards, I had just enough time to grab him by the hand. In my shock, I started shouting at him and told him never to bother me again. He looked at me, almost in horror, and that was it. After that incident, he teased and mocked everybody around him except me. When he was in that state, he passed me by as if I was not there. He did not even look at me. When he behaved normally, he spoke to me in natural cadences, and it did not seem that he had any problem with me.

All this made me think. I started to believe that his odd behavior was just a psychic outburst, so I decided to conduct an experiment. I knew that he was a fanatic concerning the icons and that he wanted us to break all relationships with the council and the whole church. He was perhaps the most fanatical in the entire monastery on this issue. So, on one occasion, when he was being unreasonable and doing odd things, I asked him if he had read the latest article from Mr. X, a scholar who supported the opposing side. As soon as I showed the article to him, he stopped behaving erratically, took it in his hands, started to read it and spoke normally.

Nevertheless, I do not think he deliberately acted irrationally. That behavior arose from him spontaneously. Perhaps his brain could not cope with the tremendous pressure that derived from the belief that your path was the only one that led to eternal life. How could it cope with the belief that one mistake, one wrong decision, and you would be punished eternally? But to their credit, the monks tolerated such behavior because they believed that it was not the person's fault but the work of the spirit that controlled him. Otherwise, they would have prescribed drugs or gotten rid of him.

One day I was in the workshop in which we made icons with two other monks, my teacher and my fellow novice monk, the "fisherman." While we were working, we used to take turns saying out loud the prayer to Jesus: "Lord Jesus Christ, son of God, have mercy on us." It was not easy to keep your mind focused on prayer while doing such detailed work. Everything had to be done mechanically. Suddenly, when it was the other novice's turn to say the prayer, he spoke in a very strange voice, as if he were mocking and being ironic. He behaved as if he was childishly trying to make us laugh, which was totally improper, not only for a monk but also for the workshop environment. Suddenly, he stopped just like he had started. He looked at us and asked: "Did I really do that?" I was shocked, because I suspected what might have happened. It seemed that we'd have to deal with two brothers with similar issues after that day, the tall one and the "fisherman."

Having conducted my behavioral experiments with the tall monk, I tried to talk to the "fisherman" and tell him that perhaps there was a chance that everything was just in his mind, a response to some pressure he felt and that his behavior was involuntary. However, he was offended because he thought I believed that his behavior was deliberate, and he was just pretending. However, that was not the case. I just suspected that his behavior was a defense mechanism he spontaneously fell into, to release the psychological pressure he felt.

Anyway, I finally got used to his outbursts, and we carried on with our lives. We went fishing together, we worked and talked. It was only occasionally that he changed his voice and said odd things. Fortunately, his condition was not as serious as that of the other monk. I became so used to it that I found it surprising when visitors were alarmed by his erratic behavior and nonsensical speech, replete with weird voices.

The third encounter was with an outsider. One day my elder asked us to assemble because he wanted to talk to us about a man from the outside world who believed that he had been possessed by a spirit. He wanted to come and stay with us for forty days, to fast and pray, and have an exorcism performed by the priest. My elder could have made the decision on his own, but because the incident was going to affect us all, he thought he should ask us whether we agreed. It was not an easy thing for the monks to have a worldly man with them for so many days, let alone a man who had psychological problems. However, we immediately agreed to his staying with us because we were used to the peculiarities of our own two "possessed" monks.

When he arrived, we were all curious to see his abnormal behavior. The only strange thing he did was rolling his eyes while still calm. During the exorcism, however, he shrieked and kicked about. That is why another monk and I were there each time to protect the priest, in case this man became violent.

Exorcism was a difficult and tiring procedure. Sometimes, we asked the man's permission to tie his hands and legs, so that he would not harm himself or the priest. Then, after he had knelt, the priest put over him the stole, a heavy ceremonial scarf embroidered with crosses and symbols, and started to read prayers addressing the evil spirit: "With the power given to me by Jesus, I order you to leave this servant of God and go to deserted dry places away from people who are an image of God." This was only one of the many prayers written for exorcism. Every time he said "leave," the priest pushed the man's head forcefully or tapped the cross on him. This was repeated many times. The man became irritated; he mocked or even swore in a changed voice. However, we never needed to intervene because he never became violent. None of the possessed became violent during exorcism.

Another time, during church service, the man shouted: "Hey you, it is true!" and froze when the priest sprinkled him with Holy Water. The difference between him and the other people that were called possessed or being tormented by an evil spirit was that he brought out some kind of evil in us. He was trying to induce discord. He would go to one person and accuse another of slandering, and then go to the other and accuse the first. Suffice it to say, he liked to mess with our peace. It was my elder's mistake that he did not send him away earlier, before one of our monks was so negatively affected that he left the monastery and went home.

I do not think that this man was pretending, just like the others. I believe that he had some psychological problems. I also believe that the others did not pretend either, but exorcism never cured them. All their problems remained unsolved. However, they usually claimed that they felt better after the exorcism. At the very least, they spent some time with other people in a different environment.

It is important to note the degree of love that the brotherhood showed on such occasions. Without any financial benefit, indeed, with the burden of feeding one more mouth for forty days and having a stranger amongst them, they agreed to it. Why? There was a chance to lessen the pain of a fellow human. That was not a singular event either. The house was always open to strangers, whether they were seeking a listening ear and shelter for a couple nights or even seeking financial or material aid.

Chapter 14. Visits

Friendship is a single soul dwelling in two bodies.

Aristotle

When we replant a small tree from its pot into the soil, we must be especially careful until it develops roots, because it is vulnerable to the air and drought. That is why I was advised not to accept visitors until the roots of my faith in monasticism took hold. And that is what I did. I had taken my role seriously, and I did not contact anyone. As a way to strengthen my determination, I did not even call my family for the first years. I know some monks never received calls from relatives, even to ask about their health. The monk is supposedly dead to the outside world, especially his relatives. My friends all believed that I was in the USA, and I had no reason to reveal the truth. That all changed when I was ordained a monk, after four years as a novice.

Because the monastery had open doors to visitors, it was inevitable that I was going to see some people I knew. The first such person I saw was almost a year after my confinement, and he happened to be my captain from the army. I bumped into him by chance, and despite my long beard and hair, he immediately recognized me. I also met some people from the churches I used to attend.

Once I started meeting acquaintances from the outside world, it was impossible to resist calling my best friend from university. Before I left, I had confided to George that he would be the only one who could find me, because we had previously visited the monastery together. Although he was somehow suspicious, he never called to confirm it. After my telephone call, he told all our fellow students, and they started to call and visit me. George was the first friend to visit me, and after that he visited every year. In fact, during one of his visits he nearly died.

We decided to climb to the top of Mount Athos, with the elder's permission. It was winter, and the peak was covered in snow. It was not the first time we had been climbing mountains together. George and I set out for the top. His boots were not suitable, but he was an experienced climber. When we reached the top, the scenery was wonderful. The wind had carved the snow, producing frozen needles that followed the direction of the wind. The clouds raced above our heads, and the frozen air smelled fresh and clean. The whole scene was enchanting, but since it was almost sunset, we had to climb down before the snow turned to ice. I had only my wooden walking stick with me, but George had trekking poles.

The descent seemed dangerous to him, so he climbed down extremely slowly. I was stressed out because the sun was setting, and the snow had started to freeze. I urged him to go faster, but he could not. About 300 feet down from the top, I heard a shout behind me: "Catch me!" I turned and saw George sliding fast on the snow. I thrust my stick into the snow and tried to catch him, but he had picked up such speed that he pushed me down, breaking my stick. I managed to stop immediately but watched in horror as George sped down the slope, generating a land slide of boulders mixed with snow. It was extremely scary. I immediately started praying and thinking about what I would say to his parents if he were killed. He kept sliding along the slope and bumping into small rocks, but I could see he was still conscious. Unfortunately, the slope ended soon, and at the end there was a sharp cliff about 600 feet tall. Believe me, I had never prayed so intensely in my life. I was terrified.

From an altitude of about 6000 feet when George started sliding, he had come down to nearly 4500 feet. Then I saw that he steered in the direction of the first tree he saw in front of him. I hoped he would crash into the tree. Then, I could carry him on my back to the cell. Fortunately, though, the ground under the tree was level, and he managed to stop! He called out that he was all right. I grabbed his poles and rushed towards him. It must have taken me five minutes to get there. Thankfully, George only had some scratches and a bruised ankle. We rested for ten minutes to get over our shock, and then continued our way back to the monastery.

Image 36 - The hike to the summit was very dangerous in the winter, but also very rewarding.

Image 37 - The slope was steep and if the snow was frozen, it was difficult to stop from a slip.

I was so relieved! I could not even imagine what would have happened if he had not stopped at that tree. I thought that, after his near brush with death, he would not want to see me again, or even talk to me, but he came again! Together, we went to the yearly celebration at the Great Lavra monastery, where more than 300 people gathered on July 18th to commemorate the passing of the founder, Athanasios (10th century AD).

After George, other fellow students from university and childhood friends came. The next visitors were three in number. It was the first time that I was going to see them since I had openly declared that I was a monk, and that made me feel uneasy. Other than that, I was so happy to see them again. Their coming meant so much to me. My friends still cared about me despite my abandoning them, and they were genuinely quite curious.

First, I took them to visit an old neighbor monk who lived with his novice a five-minute walk away from our monastery. He was born in 1924 and had first entered a monastery in 1944 at Stavrovouni, in Cyprus. In 1957, he came to Mount Athos, which he left only once in his life, in 1968, to accompany his visiting father back to the city of Thessaloniki. The first question my friends asked when they met him was whether he had ever seen a car or a television. He replied that, when he visited the city, there were still some carts drawn by horses, very few cars, and he saw a tram. As for television, he knew that it was a box that showed images, but he had never seen one. You can imagine how clear and undefiled his mind was. He was eighty-seven years old, and not even once in his life had he seen trash on television. The only thing that was on his mind was prayer. Praying is what he did his whole life. That was the advice he gave to my friends: pray, pray, pray.

Back at the hermitage, during a discussion they were having with my elder, one of my fellow students expressed skepticism about how monks could abstain from sex all their lives. How was it possible for a young monk to control his sex drive? My friend was shocked when the elder replied that a young monk must inflict pain on himself to learn to control his drives. However, I believe that there is more to it than that.

First of all, the food was free of fat. On average, we had one-and-a-half meals a day. Consequently, our bodies were probably weaker than the body of a man who ate whatever he liked at any time. On top of that, we were deprived of sleep, so there was a permanent feeling of tiredness. The most important factor, however, was psychological. In the monastery, we were a team of men with a common goal: spiritual elevation. Therefore, we had all surrendered, or tried to surrender, our will to the elder. Whatever thoughts we had, we had to confess. Because of our shame and guilt, we gradually learned to shun such thoughts. This surrender of one's will, was a spiritual castration. It was the severing of male egotism.

The same evening, we had a vigilance before the day of the Holy Ghost. My friends tried to stay up as long as they could. Of course, they had never done something like that before, so it was not surprising that they could not endure it. Only one of them managed to stay awake for such a lengthy period, which made me immensely proud. In the morning, I rested for an hour and then woke my friends. I was so enthusiastic about seeing them that sleep did not matter to me. I took them to Karoulia, which is next to Katounakia, towards the sea. This place is especially rocky and steep. There, the wildest and saintliest hermits of Athos lived inside caves, which were scattered on the cliff face, as Nobel Prize laureate Nikos Kazantzakis described. They are called Karoulia (pulleys) because access to them was possible only using pulleys, pulling people and materials up in a net. Nowadays, there are some steep trails that one must climb to get there, holding a chain for safety. We visited several caves, and I showed them the reservoirs in which, just ten years before, rainwater for drinking was collected. Now they are provided with spring water by monks from the neighboring cells.

Image 38 - A pulley helps deliver goods from the port to the Karoulia settlement.

My friends were impressed by the hard but exceedingly simple life of the hermits at Karoulia. Compared to them, we had some land to make a garden, some trees to cool us off during the hot days of summer, and stone walls to protect us from the cold in winter. They lived inside caves with tin sheets for cover. The heat was unbearable in the summer, and in the winter, it was freezing cold. It is recorded that in olden times the hermits lived there until they died. That is why the ones who live there now have a collection of human bones in their caves. Today, the hermits on average live there for eighteen months. Only one old hermit, who was still alive, had lived there for forty years, but only in the summer. In addition, there was one young hermit who lived there for eight to nine years.

Image 39 - Inside a hermit's cave. This rock inlet was used as a desk to study.

Image 40 - This part of the cave was used as a chapel, where the hermit would pray in front of the Cross.

Karoulia was a rough, imposing place which radiated holiness. As Kazantzakis described it, "A man's voice in this place seemed to be a sin to me, a sacrilege."

With all these experiences, I had a good time with my friends during their visit. They had new experiences, found answers to some of their questions, and may have taken a small sample of my life with them. They might have also learned a bit about the reasons for my choices. In that way, through these visits, I started to have contact with the world I had abandoned.

- *The hiking week*

Every year, during Easter week, according to a tradition of Athos, monks who wanted could walk around the Athos peninsula and visit other monasteries. In my first year after entering Athos, I did not do so, as I was still a novice. In the second year, I went with my icon-painting teacher, who was extremely strict. Even so, I liked it so much that subsequently I never missed the chance to get away from the routine of the monastery.

On those five days we stopped fasting and ate eggs with cheese and a traditional cake called "*tsoureki*." We were allowed to drink up to three small glasses of wine each day, which gave us great energy to cover long distances. However, we were zealots, a radical and intolerant group of monks who belonged neither to the main church of Greece nor to the Patriarchate of Constantinople. We did not want to spend the nights inside the monasteries; we sought to avoid friction with the other monks, which was inevitable because of our refusal to be in church together with them. We did not even sit at the same table because of the grace they would say before eating. So, we slept in the forest under a tree, or in a covered spot like an abandoned mill. We were free for four nights, but of course, being accompanied by a strict monk, we said our prayers exactly as we did in the monastery. I doubt whether the icon-painter slept three to four hours a day, but in any case, he was a good hiker, and we visited a lot of places together.

The next year, I received my elder's blessing to make the rounds all alone, and, for the first time in three years, I slept all through the night! It was wonderful. I said my prayers during the day while I was hiking. This time I was much more organized; I took a small tent in which to spend the night. I was so happy and felt so free that the hardships did not bother me at all. The rain, the swollen feet, and tiredness all paled compared to the happiness I felt walking free.

The year after that, I invited some friends to come with me. Three of them accepted and accompanied me on a five-day trip around the Athos monasteries. It was wonderful. We kept talking and reminiscing about our past as we hiked. One particular scenery reminded me of the mountain Kerkis that we had hiked together when we were in college, and I said:

- Hey guys, doesn't this look like Kerkis in Samos Island?

- Yes! Remember when we hiked with Philip and the other guys and got lost in that fog?

- Oh, right, we were walking for thirteen hours, that was crazy!

- But we found the Air Force shooting range and some missiles. I heard some kids got killed trying to dismantle one.

- That was so sad. Speaking of sadness, remember the airplane crash we found on the other side of Kerkis? I have a souvenir from the site, a little piece of aluminum.

- We always had such a great time together guys. Barbequing our steaks on open fire and drinking ouzo. It was such a good feeling…

I had not mentioned anything to my elder, and everyone believed that I would be alone. I believe that, if I had mentioned it to him, he would not have given me his blessing. He would have been in the right, too.

All this contact with my past made me have second thoughts about my decision to become a monk. It took me another two years of inner struggle and historical research to decide to abandon the idea of monasticism. I admit that I was the worst of monks. On the surface, I carried out my duties perfectly, but in reality, I was always looking for something different. I was hoping for concrete proof that I was on the right path to enlightenment, some extraordinary ability, not just inner peace. Not finding that led me to fill my time with other activities. Or was it the other way around?

The following year I repeated the same thing. I called some friends to accompany me again. I was going to meet them at the port of Dafne, the main port of the peninsula, and I decided to go there on foot. This was normally a six to seven-hour hike, but I completed the journey much slower than that because I visited four monasteries on my way: Saint Paul, Dionisiou, Grigoriou, and Simonos Petra. The weather was quite bad, and I feared my friends would not come. When I reached Dafne, I called them from a payphone, and they said that the ferry had not sailed because of the bad weather. They were going to spend the night in a hotel near the border between Greece and Holy Mount Athos and would try again the next morning. However, the next day the boat could not sail either. I called them again, and they told me that they would surely come the following day, but just two of them did. The third did not want to spend a second night in a hotel, waiting in uncertainty. I told them that I was going to walk up to the Zografou monastery and that we would meet there.

The rain persisted with no break, and despite my being equipped with raincoats, I was drenched. I visited four monasteries on the way, Panteleimonos, Xenofontos, Dochiariou, and Kostamonitou. I will never forget the kindness of the cook at Kostamonitou monastery. Apart from the traditional treat he gave to all the visitors, consisting of a red Easter egg with a little cheese and a slice of cake, he also gave me a jar of homemade marmalade and a whole cake because I had been walking such a long distance. The cook even gave me a dry *zostiko* robe, to change into, because mine was wet. God bless him, wherever he is.

When I reached the port of Zografou, I set up my tent to wait for my friends, who were going to come on the morning boat. It was one of the worst nights. Everything was wet, even the sleeping bag. I put my wet clothes under my sleeping bag, hoping that my body heat would dry them. As I shivered in the cold, the night seemed endless, and as soon as morning broke, I popped out of the tent to do some push-ups to get warm. I gathered my things and waited. It was not raining, and the sun came out slowly. Only some cats were there with me, and we all tried to get warm in the sun!

The sea was still not completely calm, and I feared that I was going to have to continue alone. I found a payphone and called my friends; they said they were coming. When the boat came, it was so full that the people were packed together like multicolored sardines.

I was so happy they had made it! We visited many monasteries and landmarks together. We spent the last night in my hut in the forest. I gave them the two beds to sleep on, and I slept on the ground, on my sheepskin. The next day we went up to the peak of Athos, and then we parted.

Image 41 - My friends from college, on the tour around Athos.

Image 42 - Teaching survival skills to my visitors was something I loved to do. Here I'm setting a snare under tension from a bent tree, just to demonstrate, as we would not kill animals.

That was a time when I started to feel even closer to my friends. I stopped feeling as if they were the *outsiders*, the *laymen*, the *kosmikoi* in monks' terms. Rather, they felt like *my* people, *my* friends. I started feeling like my old self again. The "dead to the world" monk started to resuscitate. It was not long after that I decided to leave Mount Athos. Perhaps my roots in monastic life had not grown deep enough after all. Or perhaps the soil of this brotherhood was incompatible with my spirit and my tree was dying.

Image 43 - A hermitage at Karoulia.

Chapter 15. New friends

It is better to be the arbitrator between two enemies than between two friends, because one of the enemies will become a friend, whereas one of the friends will become an enemy.

Bias of Priene

During the time I was on Mount Athos, I made new friendships which have lasted up to this day. May they last forever.

I met Alexandros during a hike on Athos. My elder used to send me as a guide when a visitor to our cell asked to ascend to the top. On that day, I was accompanying a priest who had visited us and had asked to make the ascent. I had a mule with me in case the priest got tired and could not walk any longer. I also had some dry food and ice-cold water with me. Alexandros was going up the slope along with a friend, Vasilis, and Vasilis's son George. When we met, I offered them some of the water, and they accepted. They were truly kind and friendly, and we started up a conversation.

About half-way through the journey, at a place called Panagia, the priest told me that he was tired and asked to rest for a while. While the priest and the boy were resting, I had a long conversation with Alexandros and Vasilis. We talked for three hours! We discussed globalization, human privacy, the explosion of technology, the economy, world politics, and history. It was a remarkably interesting discussion, and we felt as if we were a good match. We all agreed that powerful entities existed and affected global policies, influenced governments, and had secret agendas that were not always in the best interest of the masses. In addition, we agreed that personal privacy was diminishing in a world where all your data was online and handled by central entities. We also talked about history, especially the influence of the Byzantine empire on Russia as the empire's religious successor after its collapse in 1453, and then the role of Russia to the Greek people, before and after the birth of the state in 1829.

Vasilis and his son George demonstrated a closeness to and fondness for each other. I enjoyed seeing their healthy dynamic. I had been away from my father for an exceedingly long time and felt that their relationship was something I would have liked to experience. George was a very smart, six-year-old boy, far ahead of most of his peers, as I could easily have a conversation with him. Conversation was not limited to talk of toys and games, like with most six-year-olds, but rather about future plans, his relationship with his father, etc. George was disciplined and focused, not just wandering around aimlessly.

I told them that I made bows and liked archery; Alexandros said the next time he came, he would bring me a bow. Of course, I did not take much notice of it, because people promise different things just to seem kind and generous. However, after eight months, he called me and told me that he wanted to visit again with Vasilis and George and that he was bringing the bow! I could not believe how generous he was. All we had experienced together was a nice conversation, and because of that we became friends. He was coming to visit all the way from Moscow and with a present at that! Incredible!

A few days later, I went to the port with my mules to pick them up. They arrived with a hired speed boat instead of the regular boat. I was so happy to see them again! Alexandros actually brought the bow with him!

The three of them visited me many times after that. They even came with us for the celebration of Saint Athanasios in the Great Lavra Monastery.

We went to many places together, but the very last time Alexandros came on his own. He came on August 18th, 2013, a week before I left the mountain. We went to attend the celebration of the Transfiguration of the Savior, at the peak of Athos, where there is a little chapel dedicated to this event. We spent the night at Panagia with 300 other people who had come for the celebration. We had also taken with us two mules, because Alexandros was not feeling well and needed a means of transportation.

That night, something terrible happened. Another person with mules suggested that I should not take their saddles off in the evening to prevent them from catching a cold; they were sweaty. I listened to him but eased the straps a bit to make them less tight. In addition, I removed their bridles so that they could graze freely and tied them up using the chains they had around their neck.

I checked the mules just before I went to bed, but, in the morning, the bigger of the two was dead. It seems that at some time during the night the mule wanted to turn on its back. The saddle flipped over and went under his belly, making it impossible for him to get up. The ground was sloped, and the chain around his neck strangled him. It was a horrible sight. This mule was just four years old, the largest and strongest of all our mules - my favorite. What devastated me beyond his death was the fact that it coincided with my decision to leave The Holy Mount. The elders of the brotherhood took it lightly and they did not punish me, because they understood that it was an accident. As for myself, I still have feelings of guilt.

One more good friend that I made on Mount Athos was a novice monk who came and stayed in our neighborhood. At first, I did not pay much attention, because many monks came as novices, but most left after a short while. This one stayed and proved to be a very interesting character. He had met many misfortunes in his life, but this is not what I want to describe. What I will mention is that he was particularly good at making a piece of wood come to life. He was highly skilled and could make anything out of wood. For example, he made a baglama (a traditional stringed musical instrument), walking sticks in the shape of a dolphin or an eagle, and many other things.

The novice did not want to take a monk's vow; he simply lived there and helped the entire neighborhood with whatever they needed. He was the one who built the fireplace in my hut. After I left, we spoke on the phone for a little while. He tried to persuade me to return, saying that if I did, we would live together. He viewed me as his younger brother. I hope he fares well.

Another remarkably interesting visitor with whom I still keep in touch, and to whom I trusted the compilation of this book in the original Greek, is Tasos. One day, he was sitting on the veranda of our hermitage enjoying the view. He was quite a tall man with a shaved head and small slanted eyes. During that time, a nuclear accident had taken place at Fukushima, Japan. I had a magazine about conspiracies in which they claimed to have found an old card game that showed nuclear destruction. There was a clock in the background showing the exact time of the real accident. This led to a heated discussion, which later turned into a philosophical debate concerning the concept of time, how our brain perceives and interprets it, and whether it really exists in the way we grasp it. We compared Christian and ancient Greek texts on the topic of time and pointed out their differences and similarities.

We did not agree on most things, but what made the discussion interesting was that we were not trying to convince one another of the validity of our viewpoints. Each of us presented his own arguments, and if they happened to be convincing, all was well. There were no clashes of opinion - only humor and acceptance of the other's standpoint. That was something unusual for me, because whenever I discussed things with others and happened to disagree with them, they tried at all costs to persuade me that only they were right. They could not comprehend the notion that I might also have some knowledge about the topic of discussion.

We continued our discussion throughout the day, only pausing for the necessary things: prayer and food. After *apodeipnon*, the prayer at sunset, we went on with our discussion. When I looked at my watch at one point, I was surprised at how fast time had passed without my noticing. It was the time for the midnight prayer, and we had not slept at all! I had found a man with whom I could hold a conversation without prejudice or fanaticism. And he found a man who did not belong to his world and who was not concerned with the problems and worries of his society. He told me that, outside the monastery, everyday discussions were about the economic crisis and financial problems.

After this, he visited me every year, and when I left the monastery, we kept in touch and visited each other. However, as he himself had predicted, while I was still in the monastery, we were going to meet less and less. The struggle for survival deprived me of my carefree nature and eclipsed my spirituality. I do not think I have ever met another person with whom I have had such spiritual affinity as with Tasos.

Showing genuine interest in a fellow human can lead to a fruitful relationship. Living in the protective environment of a monastery cultivated a simple and genuine character in us, perhaps to the point of becoming overly trusting of people. On Mount Athos, sharing a glass of water or starting a conversation was enough to open the door to friendship. Even in the more cynical world away from Mount Athos, there are always good people looking for a genuine connection or in need of help and support. Sometimes, just holding a door or offering a friendly smile is enough.

Chapter 16. My father's visit

[The] kind of wisdom and virtue by which men order the state or the house, and honour their parents, and know when to receive and when to send away citizens and strangers

Plato – Meno 91a

I had not spoken to my father since the day I entered the monastery. He was getting older, and it was not easy for him to call from the USA. We had parted on good terms, but for some reason we just never reconnected. A couple of years after I went to Mt. Athos, my mother and brother also wanted to leave society and enclose themselves in a convent and a monastery. My mother, as a married person, needed my father's consent to leave. I don't know how she convinced him, but he gave his consent, condemning himself to a lonely life without the support of his wife in his old age. I was not proud of myself for abandoning him and will always feel guilty about that. We all left him. I had hoped he would come live with me in the brotherhood when he retired. Then, I could look after him in his old age.

Several years later, he was diagnosed with cancer on his cervical lymph nodes. The prognosis was that he had about six months to live. Even though he was still working, apparently his life was suddenly empty of any meaningful relationship. That negative internal state might have led to him giving up on life.

He came back to Greece, to be close to his relatives, but his immediate family was not there for him. His brother-in-law and niece took care of him. I am grateful to them for that.

When I heard the news of his diagnosis, I was deeply moved. I prayed hard for his health, I hoped for a miracle cure. Hope leaves last. Pandora rushed to close the box she had opened that contained all the evils of the world, but she was too late: only hope was left in the box.

My father called me one day, saying he would come to visit me. I could hardly recognize his voice. It was nothing like the vigorous voice I remembered. It was a weak squeak, coming from a shell, not a man. That broke my heart.

The priest picked him up on his way to the mountain. He visited for five to six days. I had bittersweet feelings. I was happy that my father was visiting but sad to see him so weak and skinny. I tried to persuade him to stay with me, but he had to be near a hospital. Suffice it to say, I was not thinking rationally. I just longed to be with my father for a bit longer. I gave him herbs that supposedly boosted the immune system and was hoping for the best.

A couple months after my father's visit, the priest called me aside to talk. We had returned from an all-night vigil at a neighboring skete. I thought he wanted to argue about something related to the conflict in the Church that occupied us so much at the time. But he spoke to me in a very slow-paced manner, as though he was trying to get me to deduce the outcome.

- I have some news about your father.

- Ok.

- He was not feeling very good the other day, so he called his niece, and she called the ambulance to take him to the hospital.

- Ok, so how did it go?

- Well, your cousin was following the ambulance in her car, and at some point, the ambulance stopped.

- Ok, and?

- Well, your father couldn't take it any longer.

- So, he — died?

Even though he had terminal cancer and had already lived three months more than the prognosis, and I had to expect that news at any moment, I was still shocked. As you may well know, in times of great emotional duress, the mind plays some weird tricks, clinging to any hope. After all, I had received some reports indicating that he was doing better, that some blood work showed improvements, and that some treatment was working, so I did not expect his quick departure.

That night I could not sleep. I read the book of Psalms as an offering to his soul, through my teared-up eyes. I do not know if I touched his soul, but it was cathartic for me. When it was time to get up for the routine, I felt at peace. At the time, I believed I had to abandon my family to save my own soul, to get close to God, to reach high spirituality. Now, I realize that I could have gotten closer to God by helping my father in his old age.

Image 44 – The inside of the old chapel at the peak of Mt. Athos. It was demolished and replaced by a bigger one in 2013.

Chapter 17. An end and a beginning - The decision to leave Mount Athos

Let reason go before every enterprise,
and counsel before every action

Ecclesiasticus 37:16

The decision to leave Mount Athos and abandon monastic life was not an easy one, nor one accomplished without struggle. I had to fill the gaps in my knowledge and get answers to my questions and doubts. It was far from easy to renounce the teachings of a lifetime. As long as I can remember, I was trained to believe the word of God in the way my mother's faith shaped it. I felt that I was destined to become a monk and to follow God's path for my whole life.

However, the subservience of my will and the inertia of my mind and body as a monk did not suit my character. I was not a good match for an environment preoccupied with icons. Looking back, I do not understand the reason for such fanaticism on their part. I could not rely on my elder, nor could I speak openly with him. I sometimes tried to explain my skepticism, but his responses did not help me at all. He was an exceptionally good-hearted, kind, and enterprising man, but he could not guide me spiritually. Therefore, I started studying history and ancient Greek philosophy.

I started with the *History of the Hellenic Nation*, a 24-volume edition written by Konstantinos Paparigopoulos and published in 1853. It was kept in the monastery's library. It begins with Ancient Greece, goes on with the classical period, Byzantium, the Ottoman Rule, reaching up to the creation of the new Greek State in 1828. Through this narrative, a different image of the church and its struggles started to take shape in my head. The emperors, patriarchs, bishops, and generals had a human side, made mistakes, were not just "saints," as depicted in the religious texts. More importantly, I understood the political motives of the emperors that seemed to go against the Church, because more context was revealed. They were trying to save the kingdom by striking alliances with other nations and had to compromise some religious doctrine.

Next, I read the *History of the Byzantine Empire* by Charles Diel. I borrowed it from a neighbor monk. Reading this history, I was shocked but also made aware of the evil nature of the humans who struggle to obtain power in the palaces. I learned about queens who poisoned their husbands to put their lovers on the throne, and about Byzantine emperors marrying daughters of other kings just to form alliances. These were facts not generally known because they were not taught at school (which is still often the case), and because most people do not read history.

At that point, I developed a passion for history. I obtained an eBook reader, which was the easiest way to have access to any books I wanted. I then took on the challenge of reading, in ancient Greek, the history written by Xenophon. At first, I had to consult a dictionary quite often, but I improved. I went on to read the biography of Alexander the Great by Flavius Arrianus, which was easier, as it was written in the Koine dialect. Reading history helped me realize that we must consider the context of the era before rushing to conclusions. We cannot judge actions taken by a historic figure through the morals and thought patterns of modern times.

After history, I transitioned to philosophy. I read almost all of Plato's works, in the original Classical Greek. I was filled with awe and admiration for Plato's dialogues because of the way in which he directed his fellow speaker. In these works, Plato discussed a subject with one or more people, directing the conversation so that the fellow speaker perceived the subject in the manner Plato wanted and eventually provided the answer to the original question. This meant to me that we have answers ourselves, more than we give ourselves credit for. However, we need to keep asking the right questions to get to them. We must engage in introspection and guide our subconscious mind to find answers. I even read Heraclitus's quotes, which were very hard to comprehend, but still give the brain a workout.

Once I started expanding my reading horizons, I could not stop! I read some Chinese classic philosophers, like Sun Tzu's *The Art of War* and Lao Tzu's *Tao Te Ching*, as they were already loaded on my device in English. I also read some Russian literature, like *Crime and Punishment* by Fyodor Dostoevsky, along with some political tracts, like Karl Marx's *Manifesto*, and even Adolf Hitler's *Mein Kampf*. My horizons had expanded so much that I wanted to sample everything! I no longer trusted other people's opinions. I had to see for myself. Therefore, I wanted to consult the source of a theory, not rely on secondhand reports or hearsay, and I wanted to listen to both sides of an argument.

Ironically, the final blow to my old belief system came from reading the *History of the 7 Ecumenical Councils*. It was a huge tome, printed in the 1800s by a nearby Skete, a monastic community of a few huts by the name of Prodromou. The fonts looked almost as if they were handwritten.

The minutes of the first Ecumenical Council, which took place in 325 AD, were saved by Eusebios of Ceasaria (260-339) and Gelasius of Cyzicus (about a century later). A particular story captured my attention, because it sounded so familiar to a story from another book, the *Synaxarion*. That book (usually published in twelve volumes) contains the biographies of ancient Christians and their deaths by persecution, but it is full of supernatural stories and miracles, literary embellishments. There are various editions, but they are all what the name implies: a collection from various sources.

Reading the story from the original source made me realize that a conversation between two people in that Council, who were arguing about a subject, had been changed over the centuries. In the *Synaxarion*, the same conversation was infused with folklore and became a supernatural tale, with fire jumping out of a brick and other additions. That is when I realized that I had been indoctrinated with untrue stories from my childhood, and that those stories had led me to the decision to become a monk. There were stories about martyrs unscathed by fire, and soldiers getting tired of cutting up and slashing them without effect on their bodies, or consumption of poison without ill effects etc. However, I still maintain that believing is powerful, and that the brain can force the body to withstand higher than normal situations or shut off pain.

One similar reading was a passage from Lucian of Samosata (125-180AD) concerning the burning of a Christian bishop by the state of Rome. He maintained that the other Christians who watched the execution believed that the old bishop did not burn at all, that he was unscathed by the fire. However, Lucian went to see the body, and it was completely burned. The Synaxarion has a similar story from that same era, but it has a different name. It maintains that the body was unscathed. Although there are concerns about the accuracy of Lucian's account because his writings were designed to amuse the reader, it made me think that maybe none of the other supernatural stories were true, either. I wondered why someone had added false embellishments to an account of a significant event. As if dying for your belief was not powerful enough. This was especially so if you had the choice to denounce your belief and have your life spared.

I also wondered how our beliefs could alter our perception of reality. Were people really seeing with their eyes what they wanted to see, through the power of believing? Was it real for them, but not for the rest of the world? This idea is a recurring leitmotif in literature, someone "seeing" a spirit, or a demon, while no one else does so.

In addition, I came to realize that people from different nations and cultures see the same things through different lenses. Add to this the passion to lead and not to follow, coupled with the big ego, and you have the establishment of different churches and denominations. Therefore, the clear word of God became apparent to me, as opposed to the teachings of intolerant people who promoted discord to their own advantage. I could follow the word of God anywhere, not only in the confines of a monastery, and I did not have to force myself to believe unbelievable things. Now I could practice only what made me a demonstrably better person, without fanaticism, and with an open mind.

Having all this in my head, I received a phone call from a childhood friend who wanted to visit me the following weekend. I grabbed at the chance and asked him to save a little space in his car for me and my things, because I was leaving with him. At first, he did not realize what I was saying and thought I was going to visit my hometown of Litohoro as a monk. However, I cleared up the misunderstanding, saying that I was giving up monastic life. This was something that made him happy and made me think I had made the right decision. Immediately after that, I called my aunt and asked her to get my mother's house ready for my return. My mother and brother had joined a convent and monastery in 2008, two years after my own confinement, so the house was deserted. My aunt received the news with mixed feelings. She was a religious woman, but not to the degree my mother was. She valued family and was more reasonable.

I knew that the house was empty. My mother had been trying to sell it, and she had hired people to take everything inside away. They had even taken the inside doors! That did not matter to me at all, however. I was determined enough even to sleep on the floor until I found work and was able to stand on my own. It was not going to be easy because of the economic crisis in Greece, but I did not care. It was fortuitous that the house had not been sold because of the crisis; now I had somewhere to stay.

From the moment I decided to abandon monastic life, I could not have peace of mind until I left. Everything seemed so boring. A monk's life is hard, so the hardships I was going to face out there, like sleeping on a floor, would be easy.

The same day I announced my decision to my friend, I called my mother to announce my decision. When I told her the news, she did not seem surprised at all, because, as she had told me, she expected I would do such a thing. She said that she had sensed it through our telephone conversations. I also let my brother know, and asked him not to say anything to anyone, because I wanted to be calm those last days on Mount Athos. I did not want to have them all trying to change my mind.

My brother was devastated by the news. He literally burst into tears. From what I learned, I was his role model, and he was immensely proud of me. He always talked about me and life on the Holy Mount. As for himself, he had entered a monastery close to a city. I tried to explain to him that each person was responsible for his own life, but he would not listen. He told me that he would come to Athos to dissuade me. Even though I had asked him not to do it, he was there the next morning. He had driven all night and had found a way to get on the boat without the necessary permit. My brother had also taken one of the elders of his monastery with him.

I was planning to announce my decision to the brotherhood on Friday night to avoid their preaching, but my brother came on Tuesday morning. The first one to learn I was leaving was my elder. We were all sitting on a bench; my elder, my brother, his elder, and I. As soon as I realized that my elder did not know the reason for their visit, I explained to him that I was going to leave Athos and go back to the world. He did not say anything, he just let a tear flow out of his eyes and disappear into his beard. Then the other elder tried to say something, but I interrupted him, stating that since I had been listening to them for seven-and-a-half years already, there was nothing they could say that was going to change my mind. I also asked what he thought he could tell me that I had not already heard before. After that, I heard no more preaching, only a few remarks from the other elders of the brotherhood. The rest of the monks, other than my brother, who was trying to dissuade me in any way he could, did not say anything.

I had made up my mind. I had proved to myself that I was not suited for seclusion. All I needed was to feel good about myself, which I definitely did. At that point, I felt the monastery had become a prison for me. I was choking. I had to get out of there. While I lived on the Mount, I met several monks who wanted to leave but were afraid to do so. When you suppress yourself, inevitably your body will suffer, and that is evident in your behavior and the way you speak.

The days passed painfully slowly. My brother persisted in trying to change my mind. At last, Saturday dawned. I went down to the harbor to welcome my friend. He arrived on the morning boat, and we were to leave in the afternoon. There was silence in the monastery. A kind of hush prevailed, different from the normal one, which was strange. None of them had imagined that I had thought about leaving because I had always been punctual and effective in my duties. I never openly let on that I was going to leave. Nobody said a word. They all looked at me in deep silence. I think that their greatest concern was my salvation. According to their convictions, if I did not repent and return to become a monk again, I was going to be eternally damned. What they all told me when it was time for me to leave was that they would be waiting for my return.

One of them did not even shake my hand to bid farewell. When I tried to kiss his hand, as was part of the tradition, he pulled it away, saying: “It is not necessary. You are going to recognize your mistake and come back.” Later the same day, I learned that he regretted not seeing me off properly.

The rest of the monks bid farewell to me normally, wishing me well and, of course, expressing the hope that someday I would come back. Then, my friend and I set off. Only one of the monks came to the port to see me off. This was a truly kind soul, and a good friend I had made in the monastery. I believe that he was the only one who really felt sad that I was leaving. Now he was going to be left behind. Despite disagreeing with my decision to leave, he saw me off with kind words that I felt came from his heart and soul. On the other hand, my brother, my own blood, sat a few hundred feet away without even looking at me. He listened only to his totally obsessed heart and did not come to say good-bye to his own brother. That was the last time I saw him. After that I called him a few times to see how he was doing, but that did not go well at all, and as a result I stopped calling him. He did not even respect my wish to be addressed by my original name and kept calling me Father Klimis. I hope my brother is faring well.

Image 45 - After sunset comes sunrise, after an end comes a new beginning.

Image 46 – The talandon (foreground) was hit with a hammer to produce a rhythmic sound. Skete Agias Annas.

Image 47 - A well with an attached sink.

Chapter 18. A new life

The hour of departure has arrived,
and we go our separate ways,
I to die, and you to live.
Which of these two is better only God knows.

Socrates in Plato's Apology, Sec. 42a

The car was packed. I even brought some aloe plants that I took care of in the monastery. My first experience inside a car after seven years was horrifying. On the highway, no less! All those lights, the horns, the exhaust pipes, and the noises were too much for a mind used to quietude. I was used to the peace of the Holy Mount, having the sun as light, and listening to the twittering of the birds and the breaking of the waves. I was shocked! It took me several weeks to get used to it.

On our way, there was another friend's house. His wife was a hairdresser. So, I asked my friend and driver to make a short detour for me to get a haircut and a shave. It was my first haircut after seven years at the Holy Mount. I suddenly looked like a regular citizen. At least on the outside, because on the inside I was still a highlander, trying to adapt my behavior towards other people, and especially towards women. That may seem odd to you, but being secluded in the monastery for seven years, I had forgotten how to behave in the outside world. We came into contact with people on Mount Athos, but it was not the same. Our relations were totally different, and often almost nonexistent. I did not speak to whomever entered the monastery, only to very few who aroused my interest.

My uncle and aunt welcomed me to the house. They had placed a bed, and they had connected the electricity and the water. That was much better than I had imagined. I had expected that I was going to sleep on the floor, without electricity and water, and that I was going to look for a job that would allow me to find another house to live in. What I found, though, was much better than the cell I was used to, despite the missing doors!

My first job as a free citizen was at the furniture manufacturing business of my cousin's husband. The pay was low, but then again, the Greek economy was so poor that I thanked God that I even had that. Besides, I preferred working for no money to being idle. My cousin's husband proved to be a good teacher for me. He helped me integrate into society faster. He also introduced me to people, taking me out to parties. I felt as if he were my elder brother. I could tell him everything, even about my dates. I am really grateful to him.

Speaking of dates, I must confess that, at first, I was obsessed with sex, the physical aspect of the relationship. It was probably natural after being confined for seven-and-a-half years in a monastery, consciously shutting out any thoughts related to physical pleasure. It was also natural that the relationships did not last long. A few weeks at first, followed by a few months, finally followed by a couple years. But I still did not realize the important role that giving plays in an intimate relationship. I had never allowed myself to get into another person's shoes, to feel their feelings, to answer their needs. I was still in free-running mode, as if I were released from a prison, and I had to catch up with everything I had missed out on.

I was not content with my life. I wanted something more. Everything was all right, in fact, much better compared to the monastery, but I continued to live in a small town. Everything changed when I got an invitation from an old friend from the army. He wanted me to visit him in London. This was a great culture shock for me. I wanted to live in a city like that, but I felt that I was not yet ready for such a great change in my life.

After living in Litohoro for seven months, I found work in Thessaloniki, the second largest city in Greece. It was a job related to computer programming, which I had studied at university, so I seized the opportunity. The money was not bad compared to other jobs in Greece at the time. The fact that I was working in an office with other people of my age helped me to fit in faster. I was incredibly lucky to have a chance to work in a small office with the best people I could imagine. We are still friends, and I hope to stay in touch with them forever.

That same summer, Alexandros invited me to Moscow, where I spent two wonderful weeks. Life in Moscow gave me the drive to want to do something more: to go after a better life. Alexandros always told me that American citizenship made it possible for me to seek my fortune in the United States rather than in the staggering Greek economy. First, I had to build my confidence.

Finally, after two-and-a-half years in Thessaloniki, I moved to Seattle, Washington. I decided to abandon my country and went to America in search of a better life. I had substantial help from Alexandros, who introduced me to some people he knew in Seattle. Seattle seemed an ideal place to find a job in the technology field.

A few days before I left, I received a call from a friend who visited the brotherhood quite often. He told me that my elder was in Thessaloniki to visit his doctors. While there, he had had a very serious accident caused by a faulty valve on the gas stove in the apartment he stayed in. He was seriously burnt and had to be rushed to the hospital. Although we had not spoken in over three years, I felt the need to go and see him, especially now that I was leaving the country and he was on a sickbed. We had lived together for seven-and-a-half years. I had confessed to him hundreds of times, and I had confided many of my thoughts to him. Despite our incompatible characters, he was my elder, and I respected him very much. I believed he would be glad to see me.

I had plans for that night, so I put off my visit to my elder for the next day. That evening, my friend called again and told me that my elder had passed away. The burns were too severe.

Even if I had gone there that evening, I might not have seen him alive, but I would have made the effort. Perhaps, I deliberately chose to go ahead with my plans rather than visit him. Maybe I was afraid of the awkwardness. I will never know but will always wonder.

Epilogue

"You are the average of the five people you spend the most time with."

Jim Rohn

Leaving the safe harbor of the monastery, where people were true, simple, and good, and entering the jungle of our society was not easy. Seven more years have passed, and now I have a family that I am responsible for, with a lovely and kind wife, an amazing son, and a baby daughter. I can now say that I have learned a few things.

The hardest part was choosing whom to befriend and from whom to stay away. Living in a secluded society made me become very trusting of people, believing that everyone is good deep down. That can be extremely dangerous, especially with people who befriend you just to take advantage of you. For example, the priest used to evoke a metaphor, and now I realize how true it was. A person with stained clothes cannot stand the people around him with clean white clothes. He wants them to be as dirty as himself, so he does not feel like an outlier.

By observation, we can avoid mistakes other people make. Just as a good investor invests other people's money without risking his own assets, so we can use other people's experiences to make decisions for our own lives. By watching the people around us, we can observe that certain lifestyles lead down paths that we may or may not like. Observing and processing what we observe can help us decide what path we want to follow and what people we want to have in our circle. I have made many mistakes and learned many lessons, and in the process, I have found that some core values I was taught in the monastic society, such as discipline and service, also apply to worldly society. Even without retaining the religious awe, I kept the basics to benefit my daily life.

I know that I did not achieve the spiritual heights I dreamed of when I decided to become a monk. I know now that I was not a good monk by the standards of their society. But those seven-and-a-half years on that mountain, without electricity and running water, shaped my character. I do not get angry as often and as easily as before I went there. In addition, I try not to waste time. Even when I do, I sometimes have a sense of urgency inside me, pointing out that I am wasting time.

Of course, we never stay the same. "*Panta Rhei*" as Heraclitus put it, i.e., everything flows, always changes. We are continuously influenced and changed by our environment. Having been taught those foundations of morality at Mount Athos has helped me steer away from trouble, or to get me out of trouble after a tumble. The war is not over until the last battle, of course. But, having a goal and aiming at it helps put your life back in order whenever you catch yourself slipping.

I sincerely hope that the reader found something of value in this book. My point is that people can improve their lives by the decisions they make. The values I learned on Mount Athos help me with my life, help me become a better version of myself. I believe that by sharing my experiences I can help other people, too. By setting a goal, by not wasting time, by being humble and learning, by being truthful, by loving our fellow humans. Even when we know that something is right, we tend to forget as we become overwhelmed by the activities and necessities of everyday life. Reading about how different individuals came to their particular path in life can strengthen our convictions and create a path that will enable us to become what we believe we are capable of being.

***

I will add a note about my relationship with my mother here just to point out the power of believing (in this case in a negative way) when adhering to strict uncompromising religious beliefs.

At first things were good. We would talk on the phone, but she always tried to make me change my mind and return to Mt. Athos. It was annoying. At some point I asked her to transfer the ownership of our house to me, to avoid legal troubles with her convent in case of her passing. She had no use for the house, as she would never leave the convent because of her vows. I did need it, as I wanted to establish my position in the world, plan for a family, etc. I already had started a mushroom farm in the basement and had more plans. It also served as a vacation home when I visited Mt. Olympus on weekends and holidays.

But she would not consent, thinking that it would be a "safe house" for me, giving me a reason not to return to Mt. Athos. She thought that if she could make my life in the secular world difficult, I would go back to monastic life as a "solution." But that only strengthened my resolve and helped me decide to move to the USA, as I had no reason to stay in Greece.

After I moved to the USA, we had some conversations, but they ended when we argued about who had to pay the property taxes for the house in Greece: she as the owner, or I as a tenant for two-and-a-half years. I would have sent her the money if she did not consider it a religious obligation for me: the money that the monastery had to pay was "sacred," and they would never have had to pay if the house were abandoned, and I had not initiated electricity service. My defense was, "It is your house, and you have to pay property taxes, like all other citizens. I was just a tenant. If you gave me the house, I would have paid the taxes."

Three years passed with no communication between us. My wife and I even visited Greece twice, once with our son, her grandson, but we never even talked, let alone visit. From time to time, I received a few weird calls from her people, who wanted to talk to me about religion and the "truth," but I ignored them.

Finally, I got a call from her. She was in the hospital with a badly broken leg. She had fallen from a ladder while serving at their hospice. Her attitude had changed completely, and she wanted to apologize for her harsh attitude and silence. She said she felt she had come close to death, and she did not want to leave this life with bad blood between us.

Of course, I forgave her - she is still my mother. I introduced her to my wife and children, and she was extremely happy. It was an unexpected change! She was careful not to harangue me any further where her ideology was concerned, and we could have normal conversations about our respective lives. It feels as if a huge weight has been lifted from my conscience. Now, I call her from time to time, and the interactions are positive. I wish I could do the same with my brother.

Glossary

Apathia: A state of being where the individual has managed to "clear his heart" completely of sins and addictions and has been united with God. The person is said to receive various "gifts" from God, or to uncover hidden abilities of the soul. Some may be at absolute peace with themselves, feeling unconditional love for all, healing (self or others), foreseeing the future or faraway places, high levels of wisdom etc.

Dokimos: A person that has entered a brotherhood with the intention to become a monk. He tries to determine whether the lifestyle fits him, and the brotherhood tries to determine whether he is a good fit for them and compatible with everyone.

Epanokalimafho: Ceremonial head cover, with the main cloth reaching to about the waist, and with two strips hanging on each side. These symbolize an angel's wings.

Kafsokalivia: One of the places that make up the "desert of Athos," which literally means "burn the hut." It is named after the practice of hermits burning down their huts or cabins so that visitors could not find them to bother them.

Karoulia: One of the places that make up the "desert of Athos," named after the winches they use even to this day to transfer goods over the sea to the steep cliffs of this inhospitable wilderness.

Katounakia: One of the places that make up the "desert of Athos," 1000 feet above sea level, where the narrative takes place.

Kerasia: One of the places that make up the "desert of Athos," located on a plateau with level, fertile land. The origin of this name is most likely from the word "girl" (korasio) and not from cherry (kerasi). There is a pagan altar of sacrifice that is located there from ancient times, where allegedly girls would be sacrificed.

Kneelings: A short prayer that was accompanied by performing some movements: first the symbol of the cross on your body, followed by kneeling and touching the ground with your forehead, before standing back up. It was a way to energize the body after waking up in the middle of the night, and a good exercise after 100-150 repetitions. It also worked subconsciously towards humbling yourself in the presence of God.

Kosmikoi: A term to describe worldly people who think only about everyday life and do not prepare for an afterlife. Their way of thinking was called *kosmiko fronima* by the monks and was to be avoided, as the antithesis of the monastic mentality in three ways: it emphasizes pleasure over chastity, power and wealth over poverty and humility, and assertiveness and self-confidence over obedience.

Liturgy: A service that lasted about an hour and a half and required a priest to perform it. It was mostly chanting, and it was very ceremonial. The priest would make short prayers, and the chorus (choir) would answer. It ended with the commemoration of the Last Supper of Jesus and the Disciples.

Ninth day: A term used for a day when there was only one meal served, on the ninth hour of the day, or three hours before sunset. The food was very simple and fat free those days.

Pankinia: Is derived from the words "all" and "community." It is a tradition in which one summons all the strong and able people of the area to help build a structure. Thirty to forty people would set aside their differences and work together to build a cistern or pour cement on a yard.

Schism: A division of a church into at least two parties that will not have any spiritual relations henceforward. In theory, it happens when there are opposing views, but often it has to do with ambitions and politics, and the views are used as an excuse. In the worldly sense, lawyers love them, as it results in significant court action dealing with the division of the properties.

Synaxarion: Literally means collection. It contains the biographies of the saints, usually grouped by the day of death, collected from different sources and authors. Each month has its corresponding tome in the Synaxarion. The biographies are riddled with supernatural events and miracles. The majority of the stories contain gruesome descriptions of the tortures the saints suffered from the government (usually the Roman Empire) to force them to denounce their faith, which they refused, thus voluntarily accepting their deaths.

Thelimataris (pl. thelimatarides): A person, usually a monk, with a strong ego who cannot stay under the rule of a brotherhood or even a single elder and wanders off to live on his own. Sometimes it also applies to subordinate monks that are not obedient.

Typikaris: The monk responsible for the order of a ceremony. He calls upon the next monk to read, chant, or perform another service. It is usually done in order, but considering each individual's strengths or weaknesses, likes and dislikes.

Vourdounaris: The person responsible for the mules and for transferring goods using mules.

Zealot: A person who does not accept the authority of the main church of Greece, or the Ecumenical Patriarchate of Constantinople. Usually, they do not even accept zealots from other denominations as equals. They do not have prayer in common, and they do not partake in services, especially not in the commemorative breaking of bread done at the end of a mass. They do not greet a non-zealot by kissing their hand, as is custom, but by bowing slightly from a distance, and saying "Bless you." The most radical of them believe that they are the "real" and only Church of Jesus and that all the rest of humanity is damned.

Goal of Christian life - knocks + up again
straighten up.
trial taken
to God.

Normative path to salvation but God can do what s
we judge ourselves not God.
Heaven - full experience beings of God
joy in life + love
Hell - discontinuation with God, absence of.
new experience which is then lift
Process | Journey not on/off switch
"Theosis"
become gods
grace
image of God
part of god
fullness of ourselves

Buddhist
heliocentric gods as well
- well its world
Diff god

Share nature of god
across world
Bad fields interval eg.

Indiv
No possession
All shared

No instruments
...
keeping phone
Novice - phone away

Calls after while

Father Raphael

~~Serobitic~~ → common life

Orthodox ... food ...

Allocated a monastery

Never tell influence — sin

Sin to influence

Listen to God + see which way

heart falls

100, 30, 50

Academic ... one with English ... monk ...

Library Simonos Petra — huge

4000 million ... library

Potential skills for tiny minority

... icons.

Silence — curation of sound & silence ~~nature~~ + vocal.

PhD → Path ... , ... academic

~~Father Antonio~~ Novice

Monastic + ... 2 paths ...

Printed in Great Britain
by Amazon

Cell — store — in common ...

not own

2am/4am start ... before sunrise ... to sunrise

3-4 hrs

Communion for visitors + pilgrims + tourists

Few months ... own clothes.

45674689R00094